The Word Today

The Word Today

Reflections on the Readings of the
Revised Common Lectionary

Year B Volume 1

Herbert O'Driscoll

Anglican Book Centre
Toronto, Canada

2001
Anglican Book Centre
600 Jarvis Street
Toronto, Ontario
M4Y 2J6

Cover illustration: "The Nativity" by Francesco Marmitta

Canadian Cataloguing in Publication Data

O'Driscoll, Herbert, 1928-
   The word today : reflections on the readings of the revised common lectionary

Previously published under title: The word among us.
ISBN 1-55126-334-3 (Year B, v. 1)

1. Lenten sermons — Outlines, syllabi, etc. 2. Holy-Week sermons — Outlines, syllabi, etc. 3. Lent — Meditations. 4. Holy Week — Meditations. 5. Bible — Liturgical lessons, English. I. Title. II. Title: Word among us.

BS511.5.037 2001   251'.62   C00-933143-3

Contents

Foreword

At a recent conference in the Church of England, a friend gave me a copy of Michael Mayne's beautiful and thoughtful book, *The Sunrise of Wonder: Letters for the Journey*. Early in that book Mayne, who is the Dean of Westminster, writes,

> Communication is not just about finding intelligible words. It is also about giving something of your self. It has validity only if, like Edgar in Lear, we "speak what we feel, not what we ought to say."

For me, these words speak to the task of expounding the Bible today. I cannot help feeling that, if ever it was acceptable to preach or teach in a clinical and detached way, it is impossible to do so now without great cost to our effectiveness. For one thing, the times we live in — massive change, much stress — make the needs of those who experience our teaching and preaching much greater. For another, we who have the responsibility of communicating the word are wrestling with our own faith journey in ways that previous generations could hardly imagine. To say this is not to suggest that those who spoke of Christian things before us did not have their own demons to wrestle with!

For me, the heart of the above quotation from Michael Mayne is "giving something of yourself." To the degree that we are willing to do this in our preaching and teaching, we will best communicate Christ. I name our Lord lest anyone think that, when I speak of giving ourselves, I am suggesting that we talk about ourselves. Rather, I am hoping that we will teach and preach in such a way that others may realize that we have tried honestly to hear what the scripture is saying to ourselves. This is still necessary even if scripture has not so much given us neat and ready answers as it has made us face challenging questions.

I hope you will find in these pages that I have tried to do this. In them I am not so much indicating the way you should go with a scripture, as I am encouraging you to find your own way, both of us always under the discipline of scripture and the guidance of the Spirit.

Every blessing to you in your ministry.

Herbert O'Driscoll

First Sunday of Advent

Isaiah 64:1–9
Psalm 80:1–7, 16–18
1 Corinthians 1:3–9
Mark 13:24–37

Weavings

This new Christian year starts with strong readings marked by intensity of feeling. We can feel the intensity ourselves if we are aware of the circumstances in which the words were spoken or written.

The first reading is Isaiah's anguished appeal for God's acceptance of the people of Israel, and the psalm is its echo. Paul opens his epistle on as positive a note as possible for such a difficult audience. The gospel passage is a stern, even chilling, warning from our Lord.

Reflections

First Reading

If we could be transported back to the Jerusalem of this passage to meet Isaiah, he might greet us with a bitter and weary comment: "I'm glad you can recognize this city. I can barely recognize it myself."

The people — Isaiah among them — have come back from exile in Babylon, and what they find is appalling: the hollow shell of a city. The walls are damaged almost beyond repair, and squatters from the surrounding tribes occupy the crumbling buildings. Everything that was precious has been smashed. The task of restoring the city is, to say the least, daunting.

As I read this passage, I see Isaiah taking a solitary walk through the ruined city. Perhaps it is not his first reconnaissance walk. Perhaps he is deliberately forcing himself to face the ghastly reality they have found. I see him walking until he is well outside the city boundary. Out here, perhaps on some hillside or in some secluded wadi, he raises his hands and lets out all his feelings in a shout to heaven: *O that you would tear open the heavens and come down.*

The returned exiles and their God have much to say to one another, and Isaiah sees it as his role to be the bridge between them. He expresses not only his own feelings but also theirs.

First he brings to mind the great things that God has done for this people in the past. Maybe the image of the mountains quaking recalls the days in the wilderness around Mount Sinai.

Second, he recognizes that God is a moral God before whom behaviour is always to be judged. God works for those who wait for him. God meets those who gladly do right. Relationship with God is not without conditions and demands. If God is a moral God, then a moral response is to be sought in those who would claim to be God's people.

Third, he confesses to God. I see Isaiah bowing his head, probably shaking it sadly. Perhaps he looks back towards the city. Through tears of frustration, weariness, regret, and disgust, we hear him vent his helpless anger at the situation they are in, at their own responsibility in bringing it on themselves, and at the general tragic nature of the human condition. Each admission is dragged unwillingly from him.

We have all become like one who is unclean,
and all our righteous deeds are like a filthy cloth.
We all fade like a leaf,
and our iniquities, like the wind, take us away.
There is no one who calls on your name,
or attempts to take hold of you;
for you have hidden your face from us,
and have delivered us into the hand of our iniquity.

Notice how the last line unflinchingly accepts responsibility. Isaiah is not whining like a whipped dog. He places his humanity before God and fully acknowledges responsibility for the damage done by his own human nature and that of his people.

Maybe that acknowledgement is what makes possible the extraordinary change in the next moment. I see Isaiah straighten up, look upward, and address this same God in an utterly different way. He has called God to mind. He has recognized God as a moral God. He has confessed the corporate sinfulness of his people. Now, in full awareness of the age-long covenant between God and this people, Isaiah is able to turn from confession to self-offering. Somehow he knows that, although all he has just said is only too true, the covenant still stands. Unworthy as he and the people are, the offering of themselves is still acceptable. In this moment of self-oblation he sums up what he believes about this God: *O Lord, you are our Father.* Above all, God is loving. We are the clay; God is the potter. God is able to work even with this poor clay.

Isaiah's voice strengthens, gathering confidence: *Consider, we are all your people.* I see him turn. He faces towards the ruined city, and begins to walk back to it. He and the people have work to do — God's work!

It may be helpful to recap the sequence once again: (1) God is called to mind; (2) God is recognized as a moral God who makes moral demands; (3) confession is made; (4) self-offering and self-rededication become possible.

The Psalm

There is a note of desperation in these lines. God has turned away — or so it seems. Is God's turning away the result of displeasure at human behaviour? If so, the people have already been suffering the consequences — they have shed many tears. Three times the psalm appeals for God to shine in the darkness that the people feel all around them. If God does not respond, all will be lost. No less than four times they plead to be saved from what threatens them.

We may recite these lines for ourselves at a personal level. There are times when it seems as if God has turned from us and we are cut off from grace no matter how hard we pray. We may feel ourselves cut off from relationships we value. Sometimes it seems as if friendship itself is turning into dislike and even contempt. It seems that we can hear others laugh among themselves at our expense.

In our professional lives and relationships, too, we may feel ourselves to be slipping and no longer able to cope. When threatened by such feelings, we need to hear the reassurance given by both Isaiah and the psalmist, that God is present in the situation. God may seem to be absent, but that is our perception. Above all, we need to recall that God is loving, even if that love is displayed in disciplining us. The relationship between us and God is utterly dependable; it can never be broken. By this recollection we regain strength.

Second Reading

Paul's address to the Corinthian Christians — *you [who] wait for the revealing of our Lord Jesus Christ* — may be the reason why this passage is set for the First Sunday in Advent.

We in our Advent are the companions across time of those long-ago Christians. We wait once again for the seasonal coming of our Lord. For us, the particular mode of his coming is as a child, new-born and vulnerable. For those early Christians in Corinth, the mode of his coming was as a vast and powerful judge. Whatever the different modes of our waiting, we listen again to Paul as he writes to them and to us.

Paul is addressing a community that is in an absolute mess. Everything that could go wrong has gone wrong. Still, Paul takes a deep breath and begins very positively. Notice, however, his carefully chosen words. Why does he give thanks? *Because ... the grace of God ... has been given [to them] in Christ Jesus"* He does not remind them that they have utterly failed to express this grace in their community life; he just says that it has been given.

Again, he tells them that *in every way [they] have been enriched [by Christ], in speech and knowledge of every kind.* Here he is referring to the brilliance and the culture of the community. Paul does not say how these gifts given by Christ have been misused. He merely says that the gift has been given.

Think of the countless gifts in almost every Christian community you and I know — personal gifts and professional gifts of every kind. To what extent have we used them well for the sake of the God who gave them? Our Christian community may not be as riven with corruption as the Corinthian community, but considering what we have been given to work with, have we done well? If Paul were writing to us, would he have to be just as careful about his words, diplomatically emphasizing the gifts given to us by our Lord while studiously not mentioning the poor quality of our response?

Even when Paul says, *You are not lacking in any spiritual gift,* he refrains from mentioning how this richness has been used. Is this sad truth also true of us — that while we wait once again for the coming our Lord, we lack no spiritual gift, but we lack the will to nourish and to use these gifts?

Notice, too, how Paul continues to be positive as he speaks of the future. God will remain faithful, no matter what. *God will also strengthen you to the end ... God is faithful.* For us in our Advent there is the promise that the coming of the Christ Child will not depend on the quality of our service. The Christ Child will be born because God is faithful. Are we?

The Gospel

The gospel begins as far away from Christmas lights and sleigh bells as one could possibly get. Suddenly everything is coming apart all around us. Our Lord is not sounding in the least like the Jesus of popular imagination. This is stern stuff — challenging, even frightening. Once again the theme is of a coming, but a very different one than the coming of Christmas. *They will see the Son of Man coming in clouds with great power and glory.*

This gospel reminds us that two stories intertwine during the Advent season. One story is of the child born in a stable to his mother Mary. The other is of that same child, matured to adulthood, crucified, risen, mysteriously glorified in the presence of God, and returning to bring the story of creation to a consummation beyond our understanding. Our humanity stands accountable before that returning Lord.

In this moment of his ministry our Lord is speaking of these things to his disciples. The images he uses come from the long tradition in which he himself grew up. The clouds, the angels, the winds, the gathering of humanity — all are traditional images for the time when God calls creation to an accounting.

Jesus says, *This generation will not pass away until all these things have taken place.* This brief statement has caused endless arguing. Did Jesus believe that he would return in glorious majesty within that first generation of Christian faith? We will never know. Far more worth our attention is the statement that immediately follows: *Heaven and earth will pass away, but my words will not pass away.* Here is a strong and joyful truth. History will unfold, cultures change, societies rise and collapse, but our Lord's words to us will abide. They are like great gleaming rocks in the river of time and change.

Our Lord tells us where to place our energies. We waste energy wondering if and when there is going to be an end of things. But this lies in God's hands — no amount of calculating and arguing can make any difference. Instead, we are called to live responsibly in the present. No less than three times does Jesus demand that we stay alert and awake. Awake to what? To the fact that Christian life is lived in accountability to One greater than the self. This is where Christian faith clashes sharply with contemporary Western culture. Our culture is fascinated with the self as the ultimate criterion for all decisions and all actions. In Jesus' parable the servants go on doing their work knowing that they are answerable to One who will return. The same is true for the Christian.

Second Sunday of Advent

Isaiah 40:1–11
Psalm 85:1–2, 8–13
2 Peter 3:8–15a
Mark 1:1–8

Weavings

Again this Sunday, the biblical passages are rich and vibrant with passionate intensity.

In the first reading the people of God are tasting freedom after long and depressing exile. In the psalm one of their poets celebrates a time of joyful breakthrough. The epistle is addressed to early Christians experiencing a difficult and trying time when feelings are intense. The gospel passage introduces us to a person whose vivid and vibrant presence is impossible to ignore — John the Baptist.

Reflections

First Reading

Imagine a people in exile hanging on desperately to a hope that some day they may go home. Imagine their being given the chance to return. Imagine them making the searing decision to leave behind the lives that have become familiar and to journey across hundreds of miles of dangerous country. Imagine one more thing. They arrive at the city that they have dreamt of for most of their lives. They have spoken about it, sung songs about it, pictured it in their mind's eye, listened to stories told by the elders about it. Now at last they see it. But what a sight — a ghastly ruin occupied by people who, if they are not actually enemies, are unfriendly.

Isaiah tries desperately to instill resolve into this shaken people. No wonder his very first words are, *Comfort, O comfort my people. Speak tenderly to Jerusalem.*

Now he addresses the people. He is reassuring about one thing: they have paid their debt to God. That can be put behind them. The slate is clean. Now he tries to sow the seeds of a new vision. Even in this wilderness of a wrecked city the time has come to start building. If God is present anywhere, God is present here in Jerusalem. Any work done, any building restored, any street cleared will be for this same God. Every phrase he says, every image he puts into their minds, is energizing. More than two millennia later, his language is still energizing.

In the wilderness prepare the way of the Lord,
make straight in the desert a highway for our God.
Every valley shall be lifted up,
and every mountain and hill be made low....

In other words Isaiah is saying to this weary, dejected people, "With God we can do what seems impossible."

However, there is no denial in Isaiah. He shares with the people the moods that sometimes sweep him up. There are times when he feels like saying to God, "What's the use?" People's resolve — their courage, their faithfulness — can take only so much. It can fade like a flower, wither like grass. Isaiah denies none of this. As a good leader he identifies his own feelings and those of the people. He repeats the words so full of negativity and defeat: *The grass withers, the flower fades.*

Then suddenly there is an electrifying change in his voice, his stance, his whole demeanour. The next words are spoken strongly, slowly, deliberately. First the single syllable, *but* — a pause — then: *the word of our God will stand forever.* I hear a dead silence. I feel the ripple of response in the crowd. I see faces change, backs straighten. I hear a great burst of spontaneous applause.

Isaiah takes the advantage. He knows he has them. *Get you up,* he shouts. *Get you up ... lift up your voice ... lift it up, do not fear.* I suspect the crowd is beginning to sing. The rest of what Isaiah says can hardly be heard. He tells them that if they can find the energy and the resolve to transform this ruined city, then the surrounding communities — the cities of Judah — will follow suit. His last image is designed to pierce them to the depths. No image is more powerful for this people than the shepherds and the herds of sheep that once roamed these hills and filled its market places. The image is so central to their lives that they reach for it to describe the very presence of God among them.

> *See, the Lord God comes with might ...*
> *He will feed his flock like a shepherd;*
> *He will gather the lambs in his arms ...*
> *and gently lead the mother sheep.*

Many parts of today's church need very badly to be addressed in this way, not with condemnation or the laying of guilt trips. People need to hear a voice that is comforting and tender but is also inspiring. There is no need to deny that much has been lost and much needs to be built. There is no need to deny that both leaders and people are weary and even despairing. What does need to be said again and again is that God is with us whatever the situation. We possess everything that any former age possessed. We possess the word of God, the sacramental food and drink of God, the presence of the Holy Spirit of God, and the presence of the risen Christ. The Jerusalem we must build will not be the same as the Jerusalem we remember, but the point is that we should build it.

The Psalm

These lines sound like the opposite of last week's psalm. There God's face was turned away; here God is turned towards the people. God is available and accessible, speaking peace, pardoning, restoring. This people is not alone. To know with certainty that God is with them is to be transformed. Apathy is replaced by commitment, weariness by energy.

All of this is borne out in our own experience. There are times when God seems to be absent and we thrash around searching for meaning, even for a reason to go on living. But if we realize the truth, that the seeming absence of God is nothing more than our perception, then we may experience what feels like the return of God. In fact, God has neither gone nor returned. For some reason a veil has dropped between us and God's presence. No one — not even the greatest of souls — is immune from this experience. But the faithfulness of great souls teaches us to stand firm and to wait. Steadfast love and faithfulness will inevitably meet.

Second Reading

By the time this letter was being written to the early Christian communities, the price of being Christian was proving more and more costly. In some parts of the empire, there was merely what we today would call discrimination, but in other places, depending on local political pressures, there was actual persecution and even death.

The writer of this letter sounds a theme that was common among Christians at the time. What was happening in society was not as important as what was going to happen — all was to pass away. This great change would be preparatory to a divine judgement on what had been done to people. *The heavens will pass away with a loud noise ... and the earth and everything that is done on it will be disclosed.* If this was to come about, then what really mattered was how one lived in the present turmoil. One lived in anticipation of the transformation of the world as one knew it, waiting *for new heavens and a new earth.* Since one was living in anticipation of the judging of all life, then one should live with as much serenity and as much integrity as possible.

How does this sound in our ears? How did it play out in the lives of those to whom it was first written? Since human nature is human nature in any age — past, present, or future — I strongly suspect that this letter was read with very mingled thoughts. When one's children were being victimized in school, or one's wife was ignored in the line-ups of the market place, or one's own business or trade was showing signs of being affected by one's holding to Christian faith, it may not have been easy to maintain either serenity or integrity on the grounds that everything was going to disappear in fire and earthquake at some unspecified time in the future!

Undoubtedly some strong souls did show great virtue and fortitude, but we would be unrealistic to think that Christian witness was any less inconsistent then than it is today. To realize this about those early days prevents us from entertaining the illusion that Christian faith has sunk from a shining, pure, and fearless past to a half-hearted and tentative present. It has never been easy or simple to live as a Christian in society, and it never will be as long as the vision of the kingdom of God has to be sought and lived out within time and history. Great Christian lives are present among us now as they were then. Saintliness is lived out all around us, often unknown and uncelebrated. Great things of the human spirit are possible, not only in the past but in the present. Even to be aware of this can be strengthening for those of us trying to lead the Christian life.

The Gospel

Mark wants us to encounter John the Baptist right at the beginning of his book. Mark is telling us, "Look at this man. Listen to him. It is your last chance to hear the genuine voice of the long line of prophetic figures that God has been sending to us for centuries to prepare us for something greater. Now it is about to happen." *I am sending my messenger ahead ... Prepare the way of the Lord.*

Now we meet John. Even the way Mark brings him on stage is striking. John *appeared in the wilderness.* One minute he was not there and the next minute he was! This fits in with everything about John. He suddenly faces people. He is there before they can take evasive action. His style is neither gradual nor gentle. Mark introduces him proclaiming *repentance* — John believes in confronting.

To realize how powerful an effect John had, we need to be aware of a little basic geography. It is a long way from the city of Jerusalem to the banks of the Jordan. And there is a huge descent to get there and a challenging climb to get home again. To go at all required a major decision. Yet Mark tells us that people from the whole Judean countryside and all the people of Jerusalem were going out to him. Immediately we are made to realize the immense impact he was making on society. John's physical appearance, carefully described by Mark, tells us that

John was part of a movement among young men of the time; he was a Nazarite, a man of the desert, a person of contemplation and ascetic living. This would not be the first or last time that such a figure addressed a society powerfully, challenging it to think about priorities in a way it otherwise would not. The early Celtic saints of Northumberland would do this, as would Francis in his time, and Teresa of Calcutta in our own time.

The fact that so many went to listen to this strange, rather fierce, and confrontative figure says something about the society. People must have hungered for things of the spirit, wondering what could make life worthwhile and what would make possible a life lived with meaning. When they listened to John, what did they hear? They heard of someone else, someone greater. *One who is more powerful than I is coming after me.* All great Christian lives point us to one greater than themselves — Jesus Christ. That they do so is an indication of their integrity and the truth of their witness.

Third Sunday of Advent

Isaiah 61:1–4, 8–11
Psalm 126
1 Thessalonians 5:16–24
John 1:6–8, 19–28

Weavings

Throughout these readings I sense some breakthrough moments of encounter with God acting in human lives and society, enabling something essentially new to be formed.

Isaiah feels this potential in the ruins of the city that await rebuilding. The psalmist celebrates a victory that has recently taken place. Paul sounds confident that the Thessalonian community is off and running. In the gospel John is sure that a significant moment has arrived in history, bringing change and challenge.

Reflections

First Reading

The spirit of the Lord God is upon me, because the Lord has anointed me.... Every time I read or hear these words, I have a strange sense of being in the immediate presence of Jesus. I feel this because we know how immediate and significant these words became for him. I find myself wondering about that moment when he got up and read them in the synagogue at Nazareth. Were these words of Isaiah the reading set for that sabbath, or did Jesus deliberately choose them? If the former — was this the moment when they struck him as the measure for all he would do and say in the years ahead? If the latter — at what moment in previous years did they strike him as so significant? When he was a child in the village rabbinical school? When he heard them from the lips of Mary or Joseph?

For Isaiah, this moment is all important. Suddenly he feels called and energized to take on the formidable task of rebuilding. It is not surprising that he refers to the people around him as oppressed and brokenhearted, even though they have returned to Jerusalem. It takes more than a few weeks or months for the long years of oppression to be lifted from hearts and minds. A lot happened in those years to break many hearts. Even though these people are now once again free, they still need liberty proclaimed to their inmost beings. Spiritually and psychologically they are still captives and prisoners. They are still in mourning — for years lost, a country lost, self-respect lost.

I see Isaiah walking among the people as he offers these next splendid and beautiful images. I see him going to one person and saying, "I want you to have *a garland instead of ashes*"; to another, "You should feel the *oil of gladness instead of mourning*"; and to yet another, "Do you know what you need? You need *a mantle of praise instead of a faint spirit*." All the time he is speaking he is healing, comforting, encouraging, energizing, coaxing, persuading. I feel very strongly that this is the kind of ministry we are called upon to exercise with each other today — a ministry of encouraging and healing each other.

Notice how Isaiah says that the people will be called *oaks of righteousness*. Right now they are a million miles from being strong and upright. He is depicting not what they are, but what they can become and will be. Notice his deliberate use of positive language, a succession of strong active verbs, images of things accomplished: they shall *build up ... raise up ... repair ... the devastations of many generations.*

For I, the Lord, love justice. So much for physical achievements. Isaiah now turns from city building to nation building, from exterior agenda to interior, from physical to spiritual, from pragmatic to moral. It is not enough just to build buildings. The question is, what kind of a people will live in these buildings and in this city? Above all, will they be a people who have formed a society of justice? Isaiah's implication is — and this theme runs all through the scripture — that only societies of justice are strong and lasting. Now, at the turn of the millennium, the world is wrestling with the relationship between the new market economies and the need for social justice and human rights. Can a society remain viable and strong if it does not look to forming a social system that is just and caring? The biblical question stands at the centre of social planning today, as squarely as it did in a devastated Jerusalem long ago.

The Psalm

I think it would be possible to take this psalm and the two previous psalms of this season, to place them in a sequence, and to trace the rhythms of our personal relationship with God, pointing to the changes in that relationship.

As we have seen, psalm 80, set for the First Sunday of Advent, is an expression of something akin to despair. God is not to be found. There is no trace of God's presence in spite of our agonized searching and pleading. In psalm 85, set for the Second Sunday of Advent, there is a great change of mood. God has been found again! We are no longer alone. Now in today's psalm, there breaks out the sense of utter joy in being no longer alone, the joy in knowing that the relationship between us and

God has not been broken, as we feared it had been. The psalm is a shout of joy, probably even a dance.

We might turn inward, seeking times or circumstances in our own experiences when we have gone through this sequence. First, the seeming absence of God, felt perhaps in terms of the absence of joy, meaning, hope, self-confidence. Then, the realization that God is mysteriously present with us again, making it possible for us to take hold, to come back to life. Finally, the utter joy of feeling light in our darkness, joy in our despair, energy in our weariness, life in our seeming dying.

Second Reading

It is important not to hear this passage as just fervent preaching, persuading people to do something without regard for the reality of their situation. Paul writes these words near the end of a letter to the Thessalonian community. He fully acknowledges their need to face problems, even though things are going quite well. He has named those problems already. Now, before ending, he moves into an encouraging mode. It is worth examining the pattern of what Paul says.

First there are those things that are in their power to do themselves.

> *Rejoice always,*
> *pray without ceasing,*
> *give thanks in all circumstances ...*
> *Do not quench the Spirit.*
> *Do not despise the words of the prophets,*
> *but test everything;*
> *hold fast to what is good;*
> *abstain from every form of evil.*

Next Paul mentions what God can and will do.

May the God of peace himself sanctify you entirely;
and may your spirit and soul and body be kept sound
and blameless at the coming of our Lord Jesus Christ.
[Always remember there is] one who calls you....

Everything here fits our situation today in our life together as Christian communities and in our personal lives.

Take just one phrase as an example. Paul tells us that we must not quench the Spirit. This is an important warning for Western Christians. There is ample evidence that Christian faith in the West is recovering an almost lost sense of the work and presence of the Holy Spirit. Precisely because this work of the Holy Spirit defies prediction and definition, we are wary of its manifestations in congregational life, sometimes with good reason. But the fact remains that we must enable this return of the Holy Spirit to our corporate life.

Paul himself has good advice for us in this passage when he says simply, *test everything.* This means always being ready to test the work of the Spirit, both in personal and in congregational life. It means being ready to test what the Holy Spirit is saying in our own hearts, and to let others test what we are saying without becoming threatened or angry. We need to remember that the Holy Spirit is not only within each one of us, but among all of us.

The Gospel

John the evangelist, the writer of this gospel, leaves us in no doubt about the effect of John the Baptist on the society of the time. He tells us that the Jews sent priests and Levites from Jerusalem for the express purpose of questioning John. Obviously his message was seen as significant enough to check up on.

Who are you? they asked. A few years later they would be asking the same question of Jesus. John's reply tells us that he knew exactly what they were probing for. Perceiving that their fears were political, John replies quite categorically, *I am not the Messiah.* People claiming to be the Messiah were seen as a threat to peace and good order. The Romans were particularly edgy about such people who had the potential to raise up mass movements. The delegation from Jerusalem was probably still unsatisfied when John elusively couched his reply in the form of a quotation from Isaiah, *I am the voice of one crying in the wilderness, "Make straight the way of the Lord."* These words of the prophet hinted that, even if John was not threatening in himself, he was announcing the approach of something or somebody who was! In fact, John went further. The person he was referring to was already among them in the crowd around him.

The atmosphere of our own time is full of the sense of enormous changes, all of them vast and seemingly connected. We feel helpless in the face of this great transition from a known past to an unknown and rather intimidating future. John told people that they had to get ready to live in a very different kind of world. So it is for us. We are having to learn to work in a new way, to train for professional life differently, to live without past securities, to become flexible — on and on the list goes, enumerating the endless ways that we must adapt to meet the new realities that are coming — we might say, that are already here.

What does John the Baptist say to his listeners? He tells them that new spiritual demands are going to be made on them. And is not this exactly what is being asked of us as we prepare for an uncertain future? We are already discovering the need for greater spiritual awareness in order to survive new realities of the coming century. We may use secular language for what we are discovering, but in the age-old language of the Bible, we are seeing a whole culture going in search of its long-lost soul!

Fourth Sunday of Advent

2 Samuel 7:1–11, 16
Luke 1:47–55 (Canticle 18)
Romans 16:25–27
Luke 1:26–38

Weavings

When I read these scriptures, why do I find myself thinking of houses? And why do I find myself thinking of the irony or, if you will, the humour of God? Because I think I see no less than four houses here.

In the first reading there is the obvious house that David and Nathan are talking about. In the second reading Paul is speaking of the gospel, which we can think of as a home or shelter for the seeking mind and heart. In the gospel we see that the house in which God comes to dwell is none other than the womb of Mary. The psalm is her song of welcome to the one who has come to dwell within her. The irony is that God comes finally to dwell in a house totally different from the one that David envisaged — a house of flesh, Jesus our Lord.

Reflections

First Reading

This fascinating moment in the life of David as a man, and of Israel as a people, speaks to our present situation as Christians in our culture. First we examine the incident itself.

When the king was settled in his house .... This seemingly simple statement tells us a great deal. David has come to the end of one phase of his life and is beginning another. The homeless warrior — really a kind of glamorous brigand — is beginning to taste the joys of settling down. He has captured the tiny city — really a fortress — and is now ensconced in a pleasant building that serves as his royal palace.

David suddenly realizes that, while he now lives in a house, the tabernacle — the dwelling place of God — is still nothing more than a desert tent. A devout and sensitive man, he wonders if this is proper. He consults Nathan the prophet, a trusted advisor, who agrees that they should build something fitting. But that same night Nathan's mind is changed. He feels that he has heard God say, *I have not lived in a house since the day I brought up the children of Israel from Egypt to this day, but I have been moving about in a tent and a tabernacle.*

God speaks through Nathan, reminding David of his own past. Is David's wish to place the presence of God in a house connected with a settling stage in his own life? Is Nathan also wrestling with something hard to pin down but nevertheless very important? What are the gains and losses if Israel shifts its allegiance from a God present in a movable flexible tent to a God present in a house with foundations and walls?

At this stage we begin to see links to things we struggle with today. When does the institutionalizing of religious faith begin to produce more losses than gains? In our Western culture we have certainly moved God out of anything resembling a tent into countless great houses. Are we paying a price for this, now that we once again need to be freed up to discover new ways of communicating Christian faith and of forming Christian community?

Towards the end of this passage there is dramatic irony for Christians in the sentence: *The Lord declares to you that the Lord will make you a house.* In one sense, this came true when Solomon built the temple that his father David had only thought about; in another sense, this came true when a young woman in Nazareth said Yes to an annunciation made to her.

The long-ago conversation between Nathan and David continues among us now, as men and women carry out God's work in society. Sometimes small groups work quietly with a low profile. Could we call this the "tent mode" of doing God's work? Sometimes the whole church becomes involved, acting publicly or even politically. We might call this the "temple mode" of doing God's work. This is not an "either-or" but a "both-and" situation.

The Canticle

As the scene with David and Nathan fades away, a thousand years slip by in a moment, and we hear the voice of a young woman singing, a young woman ecstatically joyful. *My soul magnifies the Lord, and my spirit rejoices....*

At first her song is personal, though even here the emphasis lies beyond herself, with God. *The Mighty One has done great things.*

Now she paints a portrait of this Mighty One, the God of Israel. That she has been lifted from utter lowliness to high privilege is only another indication of what is true about this

God. This God scatters the proud, lifts the lowly, and fills the hungry, not by magic, but by calling real men and women in every generation to do these things.

Remembering the images of tent and house (or temple) in the first reading, we might observe that much of the work of lifting the lowly and feeding the hungry has to be done outside the life of the temple, by men and women who see that God can never be limited by walls. Sometimes this work on the boundary between church and world has to risk stepping out of the temple and perhaps setting up a tent in places where temples are simply ineffective!

This song of Mary tells us that God is never limited to institutions, even if they be for God's service and worship. To carry out certain plans and purposes, God is always ready to reach beyond the institution. In Mary's Jerusalem the magnificent temple is understood by everyone to be the house of God. This house is not rejected by God; it simply cannot carry out what God now chooses to do. For the sublime purpose of God's entry into the world in an utterly different way, there is needed not a temple but a human womb.

Times without number in history God chooses to work through a single human life to bring something to birth. Right now God is using our lives to bring new things to birth!

Second Reading

I am tempted to say an impish thing here. If you read this passage through quickly, you realize that Paul's punctuation is in tatters as his writing hand tries to keep up with his thinking.

This passage should have been written in verse form because it is a kind of hymn, a magnificent flourish at the end of Paul's greatest and most extended expression of Christian faith — the letter to the community in Rome. When he says, *Now to*

God, he is both giving glory to God and also handing over to God this great piece of work he has just completed. It is fitting that we read this passage on the last Sunday of Advent because he has finished just in time — the Christ whom he has been describing and commending is about to arrive in person!

Is it not ironic — and very wise — of Paul to refer to our Lord Jesus Christ as a mystery, even after he has spent endless hours expounding faith in this Lord in a coherent and understandable way? In his wisdom Paul knows that our Lord will always remain a mystery that eludes all attempts to unravel and explain to our satisfaction.

The Gospel

In the sixth month the angel Gabriel was sent by God to a town in Galilee called Nazareth. I have always felt a sense of wonder at this statement. It seems designed to confuse levels of reality. The specifics of the sixth month and a town in Galilee called Nazareth clash in the mind with the mysterious figure of the angel Gabriel. Eternity is trespassing into time. Heaven is reaching into earth. What is real here? What is unreal? Do either of these terms — real and unreal — have any usefulness in this moment of the interweaving of worlds?

I frankly doubt that they have. I am convinced that we must bow our heads in this moment and give ourselves over to something beyond and above our calculations and our efforts at categorizing.

So how are we to comprehend this moment of annunciation? How did Mary understand it? As I move instinctively from language to art in search of an answer, there comes to mind the magnificence of Fra Angelica's *Annunciation.* Gabriel is both crouched and leaning forward with outstretched arm, as if reassuring but keeping his distance, so as not to terrorize. On the other side of the room, and of the canvas, the virgin is both drawn forward and repelled by the visitor. Their eyes are locked together, as if sight alone can ask the angel's question and give the woman's response, both question and response being mysterious beyond words.

As Mary responds, we are returned into the everyday realities of life. She says, *How can this be, since I am a virgin?* It would be hard to think of a more practical down-to-earth question!

The reply of the angel takes us soaring once again into another realm of reality. *The Holy Spirit will come upon you, and the power of the Most High will overshadow you.* I suggest that arguing and analyzing have no place here.

As I write these lines, one of our children is in the last stages of her second pregnancy. Her quiet joy and serenity, in spite of a natural nervousness at the prospect of giving birth, suggests to me that the Holy Spirit has come upon her and that the power of the Most High overshadows her. Certainly my prayer for her is to this end. Her child will most certainly be holy — a child of God. The fact that the child is born of the love and passion of herself and her husband — and is also born of the God-given gifts of medical knowledge, which made it possible for her to overcome barriers to pregnancy over a long period — does not lessen by one iota the work of the Holy Spirit in overshadowing her and her child.

I do not know how Mary's womb was impregnated. If someone confronted me with undeniable evidence that the child was born of the love she shared with Joseph, I would not for a moment feel that the work of the Holy Spirit, or the overshadowing power of God, had been any the less. For that matter, I strongly suspect that the God who truly loves and rejoices in creation would have at least been tempted to use for entry into this world those elements of human physicality that God had already formed in creation.

One thing we know — Mary said Yes to giving this child birth. *Here am I, the servant of the Lord; let it be with me according to your word.* That she said Yes is the good news of this day.

Christmas Day: Proper III

Isaiah 52:7–10
Psalm 98
Hebrews 1:1–4, (5–12)
John 1:1–14

Weavings

Today's readings strive to express the glory of God's coming into the world in human flesh. In the first reading we hear the prophet explaining to the people of God what it means to be free to build their world again. This implies that, for us, the birth of our Lord gives us freedom to think and live and act in new ways. In the psalm we hear of the whole creation celebrating the mighty acts of God. For us the act of greatest significance is God's gift of the holy child. The writer of the second reading emphasizes that Jesus is nothing less than the exact imprint of God's very being. The sublime language of St. John's gospel shows us Jesus, the Christ, above time and creation.

Reflections

First Reading

How beautiful upon the mountains are the feet of the messenger who announces peace. Once again we need to put ourselves in the position of Isaiah and the people he is addressing.

As they came back from exile, they likely made their final approach towards the borders of Israel from the southeast, along the northern edge of the desert that is today southern Iraq, northern Saudi Arabia, and southern Jordan. If so, they may have looked again from the low range of the mountains of Moab and marvelled, as did their ancestors coming from the Sinai centuries earlier, at the beauty of the Jericho oasis. It may be this memory that gives Isaiah his image to open this lyrical passage.

Who announces peace, who brings good news, who announces salvation. The language of the Bible is never one-dimensional but many-layered. In every event the presence and the work of God are seen at many levels simultaneously. The returning exiles would naturally rejoice at the sight of the land they were longing for, but in the joy of that sight there is also potential peace — shalom. Their fragmented world has come together again, and they have a chance to be a people once more, possessing their own identity and integrity.

But this is not all that Isaiah sees. In this moment he sees salvation. Exile has not destroyed and obliterated them. Their identity has been saved. Their national life has been saved. Above all, their relationship with God has been saved. This is why he climaxes this statement with the shout: *Your God reigns.*

Bearing in mind the season of the year, look now at the succession of terms we have reflected upon: *good news, peace, salvation, God reigns.* Is it true that at Christmas God has come into the human story? This may seem a strange question, but as we know, we live in an age that seeks belief rather than possesses it. For us, the way forward may be to operate as if it is true that God has entered history. If so, what would follow? How is it good news?

We would realize that human history is not just a pathetic cosmic accident, a hodge-podge of events — and this would be very good news. To believe this would bring a sense of peace — shalom. Believing that the world makes sense and has purpose would give human experience and human events final meaning and purpose — and give peace to those who believe it. We would experience a sense of being saved from meaninglessness and loss — forms of exile that characterize much of contemporary life. We would have the sense of someone being in charge — God reigning.

Today in Western culture, we are in many ways returning from a time of exile — exile from faith, exile from meaning, exile from spirituality, exile from God. The evidence is in the media, in the arts, in the sciences, in people's deep seeking, in the stirrings of revival within the church. The language of this magnificent passage can be our language if we are prepared to make it so.

The Psalm

Excuse my levity, but when I begin to read this psalm I seem to hear a raucous voice shouting in a great hall, "Strike up the band!" This may not be irreverent as it sounds. Anyone who shouts, "Strike up the band!" has something wonderful to celebrate — like Christians at Christmas!

The band that the psalmist calls into being is nothing less than the whole of nature. The earth, the sea, the rivers, the hills, the world of humanity — all form the choir for the psalmist's wild outburst of joy and excitement.

Look down through the lines of the psalm to the words the psalmist sings: *a new song, marvellous things, victory, mercy, faithfulness, joy, righteousness, equity.* We are invited to look on the birth of our Lord with nothing less than the same excitement and joy. On this feast of Christmas God is saying to us,

"Look what I have done. I have come among you. Sing and clap your hands!"

Second Reading

We may never know who wrote this letter. But we do know that it was written to Hebrew Christians, people who had grown up in the long story of Judaism before deciding to follow the way of Jesus of Nazareth. The writer knew that these people would understand the images and the assumptions of Judaism.

So the writer first speaks of the prophets, showing that the birth of Jesus was connected with the long centuries of Jewish tradition. At the same time, the writer is at pains to emphasize that Jesus is not just another in the line of the prophets. Notice how the first part of the reading is a kind of creed about Jesus.

> *a Son ...*
> *heir of all things ...*
> *through whom [God] also created the worlds ...*
> *the reflection of God's glory ...*
> *the exact imprint of God's very being ...*
> *sustains all things ...*
> *powerful word ...*
> *made purification for sins ...*
> *at the right hand of the Majesty ...*

I hope I am not being unfair to well-meaning people, but as I look at this list, I realize the great gulf between what this writer is saying and what the writers of today's Jesus Seminar seem to be saying to me, of a Jesus who was little more than a moral teacher.

In the second part of the reading, the writer makes a definite separation between our Lord and angels. At this time in

Judaism there was a very widespread belief in angels as God's messengers, agents of God carrying out various tasks that often involved contact with human beings. This theme is popular again in our own time, appearing in drama and movies — most powerfully in the Broadway drama *Angels in America* and in recent movies such as *Michael*.

The writer emphasizes that Jesus is never to be regarded as just another such angel. Anything said of angels — and we are given examples — pales into insignificance when compared with what is said of Jesus as Lord. Look at the majesty of the statements about Jesus as the Christ.

> *Your throne, O God, is forever ...*
> *anointed ... beyond your companions ...*
> *founded the earth ...*
> *the heavens ... the work of your hands ...*
> *your years will never end ...*

This Jesus is much more than a handy resource for my spiritual journey. When I come into the presence of this Jesus, I don't suggest a cappuccino or a latte over which I can get therapy for my personal problems. In this presence I bow down. I acknowledge One so far above me that to try to calculate the qualitative difference would be utterly meaningless.

The Gospel

Like the writer of the Letter to the Hebrews, St. John faces the challenge of finding language to express the immensity of the meaning of God's entering human flesh.

Consider for a moment what it is that allows the prophet Isaiah to communicate confidence to the Israel of his time; in fact, to communicate this confidence in the face of fearful evidence to the contrary! It is because he himself is utterly confident that there exists a reality beyond the immediate situation itself. That reality is the ultimate reality of God.

Consider why the unknown writer of Hebrews is enabled to write in the way that he does, pointing to a future of possibilities. Once again it is because he takes it absolutely for granted that, above and around any efforts of his own, above and around any planning or actions of the community, there is the reality of God, active, transcendent, unimaginably alive.

The reason it is so important for us to realize the reality and the effect of this divine source of grace and energy and confidence is that so much in our culture denies this same reality. The presuppositions of the culture we live in do not have room for the reality of God. For many today, what exists in time and space is all that there is and within this we work. On this the post-modern world is based. Yes there are those in the sciences who are prepared to entertain the possibility of God! Yes, there is a widespread interest in what is generally called spirituality. But a great deal of this interest is in terms of inner journey into the self, and many pursue it for essentially self-centred purposes. Most of this spirituality does not think in terms of a transcendent God before whom one bows down, having discovered a self beyond one own's self — and thereby, of course, having discovered one's true self!

These passages of Isaiah and of the writer of Hebrews and are now crowned with the incomparable vision with which John opens his gospel. There is not a word or thought in these verses that views the human self as the ultimate domain of reality.

The passage begins beyond time and space. The One who comes is fully human, yet at the sasme time comes as the gift of God to humanity. This One who comes offers a light in the human darkness, a source of power for those who identify themselves with him, and a shining vision of what it means ultimately to be human.

In him was life and the life was the light of all people ...
to all who received him ... he gave power.
[He] became flesh and lived among us, and we have seen
his glory.

There is no hesitation on John's part to speak of the tragedy of our not knowing him when he came among us. In six clipped sharp words the tragedy is delineated. *The world did not know him.* Taken as a whole, the culture we live in does not know him. We ourselves have to ask ourselves if we know him! Yes, we know about him. We may be aware of the endless opinions being offered today as to who and what he was in his earthly life and who he can be today for those men and women who seek him. But do we know him as a source of *grace and truth* for our lives? Do we know him as one who calls us constantly to greater spiritual maturity? As John says — *to all who received him ... he gave power to become children of God.*

The operative word is — *become.* If Jesus is indeed Lord for me, then he calls me to a lifetime journey towards spiritual maturity.

First Sunday after Christmas

Isaiah 61:10–62:3
Psalm 148
Galatians 4:4–7
Luke 2:22–40

Weavings

In each of these passages, someone looks at a situation and more is revealed than first meets the eye.

In the first reading Isaiah is looking at a ruin and sees a garden. The psalmist looks at creation and sees the God of creation, and he responds with a shout of praise. In the second reading Paul looks at a servant and sees the child of a loving father. In the gospel two elderly people see in the child what no one else sees.

Reflections

First Reading

The people of God have come back to Jerusalem. Returning home had been their dream, but the actuality has proved to be a nightmare. There is so much damage to repair that they are discouraged and fearful.

Isaiah's voice has the ability to make a difference, to lift hearts, to build morale. But for Isaiah to achieve all this, he needs access to resources of the grace to be strong. These resources come from his powerful relationship with God. Listening to Isaiah's voice in this passage, we don't know if he is alone or talking to people around him. I am inclined to imagine this moment as a solitary one. I see him outside the ruins of the city, looking back at them.

Swept by a strong sense of vocation, he knows that God is calling him to minister to a traumatized population. He finds himself filled with the urge to speak and to act. He is almost singing a spontaneous psalm.

> *I will greatly rejoice in the Lord,*
> *my whole being shall exult in my God;*
> *for he has clothed me with the garments of salvation,*
> *he has covered me with the robe of righteousness....*

All of us have such moments, though they may not occur in a religious context. The moment we realize that someone we love, loves us; the moment we land a job that will use our gifts and stretch our abilities; the moment of physical exaltation from exercising or sports — in all such moments we exult in life, wanting to seize it and live it fully. In these moments we are conscious of receiving garlands and jewels, to use Isaiah's images. How often do we pause to acknowledge the source of all the life, all the joy, all the surging emotion, all the well-being? *I will greatly rejoice in the Lord, my whole being shall exult in my God.*

As he stands looking at the bleak prospect before him, Isaiah shows his greatness. Try bringing to mind a picture you have seen of a bombed-out city — the gaping walls of houses and factories, the piles of rubble, the human figures moving about listlessly, trying to pick up the pieces of their lives. This is what Isaiah sees. But his eyes do not stop at these sights. His inner eye sees differently — and much more.

The earth brings forth its shoots,
and as a garden causes what is sown in it to spring up ...
Jerusalem's ... vindication shines out like the dawn ...
Kings [shall see your] glory ...
You shall be a crown of beauty ...
a royal diadem in the hand of your God.

Savour this language and its images; then remind yourself again of the filth and destruction Isaiah was looking at.

We are being asked to see all of reality in a way that transforms reality for ourselves and for others. Easy to say; hard to do. Yet to the degree we can do it, we bring joy and encouragement to ourselves and to others. We make it possible to respond to tasks that challenge us, to reach for transformations that call to us to be accomplished.

The Psalm

The psalmist is looking at creation but seeing beyond it. He is not so much looking *at* creation as looking *through* it to discern its source, the creator God. Notice the very first words of the psalm: *Hallelujah! Praise the Lord.*

The psalmist's insight helps us to understand the relationship between environmental concern and Christian faith. There are many motivations for being concerned about the natural environment, beginning with the self-preservation of our species — a most valid concern. Another motivation regards the earth as sacred — and this is a great truth. But Christians go a step farther. They know the earth is sacred because it is God's creation.

Reading this psalm during the Christmas season reminds us that, in a mysterious sense, the coming of God into time and history in Christ affects the whole created order. In the great painting of the resurrection by Piero della Francesca, we see Our Lord rising from the tomb and reviving all of nature. The left side of the canvas is in the dead of winter, but the right side is in the springtime of life.

Second Reading

Paul is always probing the relationship between law and grace. For Paul, to believe in Christ as Lord relieves the burden of achieving acceptance before God by obeying the law. Paul's great insight is that I am accepted before God through the grace of Christ. I come to God through Christ.

If it is true that our acceptance before God comes through a relationship with Jesus Christ, then this relationship becomes paramount. There is no point in trying to calculate the degree to which I succeed in coming up to the standards demanded by law. My relationship with Christ defines who I am before God. To live under the law makes me a kind of slave or servant. Paul insists that our relationship with Jesus Christ has given us a relationship with God. I have become a child in the family of God, not a servant of the family of God.

All of this may seem academic and unconnected with everyday life; yet time and again we can discover in ourselves and others a sense of inadequacy or guilt because we are unable to come up to certain standards that we have set for ourselves, or that have been set for us by others, perhaps in our childhood. Sometimes the wrestling to achieve this ever-receding goal can be wearying and self-defeating. To realize that acceptance is not conditional upon our coming up to a certain standard, but that we are accepted as we are, is to feel a great burden lifted. We learn the great releasing truth that our walk to freedom begins in the realization of unconditional acceptance.

The Gospel

In my mind I am standing on the temple steps on the day when Mary and Joseph come to present their new-born child. As soon as they appear and begin to climb the steps, I follow them through the various courtyards, watching them pause to buy the two birds, seeing them join the line of other couples there for the same reason. I watch as they come before the priest who is on duty that day, and give him the child. I see him hold the child over the fire, bringing to mind for a moment those terrifying times, long before, when people fell into the practice of child sacrifice. Then I see the parents receiving the child back. In his place, Joseph hands over the two inexpensive birds, and they are sacrificed.

I watch as their going is arrested by the arrival, first, of the old man and, then, of the old woman. I see the old man carrying off the child. I hear him singing of the child's mysterious significance, then giving the terrible warning to his mother that her heart will be broken.

Now I consider those two old people, Simeon and Anna. It is they, in their old age, who have the insight to recognize the presence of God in this moment. We, too, in our older years, must seek God in the present and not merely in the past — in memory. Our prayer is to become the kind of older man or woman who can recognize the sacred Child, the holy birth, in the world of our time, in the church of our time, and even in our own selves. When this happens in someone's older years, it is beautiful to behold.

If we, as it were, "freeze" the film just at the moment when Anna returns the child to his mother, we see a very interesting scene. At the centre of everything is the child, the Christ. Around him is a group of four that represents the full spectrum of human life stages. Mary, the young woman; Joseph, the slightly older but still young man; Anna, the elderly woman; and Simeon, the elderly man. All respond to the child in their various ways.

This is the point — any time is the right time to say Yes to Christ as Lord. There is a beautiful Irish song, usually sung in Gaelic, that expresses this perfectly.

From birth to youth,
and from youth till death,
your two hands, O Christ,
stretch over us.

From death — the end?
No end — but new life.
In sweet Paradise
may we be found.

(As this hymn has a lovely tune, you may wish to be able to trace it. It was written by Sean O'Riada, 1931–71, and the translation is by George Otto Simms, former Archbishop of Armagh in the Church of Ireland. It is published as Hymn 139 in *Irish Church Praise* [SPCK and Oxford University Press, 1990].

Second Sunday after Christmas

Jeremiah 31:7–14
Psalm 147:13–21
Ephesians 1:3–14
John 1:(1–9), 10–18

Weavings

I am struck by the ways in which these passages (which remain the same for all three years) speak to the church of our time. In the first reading Jeremiah addresses Israel at a difficult moment and offers reasons for confidence in the future. In the psalm Israel is given the absolute assurance that God will bring blessing. In the second reading Paul puts before the new Christian communities a list of the spiritual riches they possess, if only they are prepared to see them and appropriate them. In the gospel we are shown by St. John how God entered and goes on entering the human situation from beyond the limits of that situation.

Reflections

First Reading

Sing aloud with gladness ... raise shouts ... proclaim ... give praise. I hear this exhortation of the prophet as a reminder to us that the church's life today requires worship rich in praise. The health of every congregation depends upon praise. So we must ask ourselves: what is the quality of our music? Can our choirs be encouraged and strengthened? Are music and singing taken for granted? Do we express appreciation for those who lead us in these activities? Are we prepared as a congregation to explore the flood of inspiration that the Holy Spirit offers the church today in new hymns?

Down through the centuries nothing has been as energizing to Christians in times of stress and turmoil — even in times of persecution and suffering — than their gathering to offer praise to God. We get a hint of this in what Jeremiah says next.

In the international turmoil of the time, life for God's people was full of fear of what lay ahead. This is why we hear the cry, *Save, O Lord, your people, the remnant of Israel.* Very often a small congregation today can feel like a pathetic remnant of a once stronger church. But notice that this cry for help is offered as a burst of praise. It is not just, *Save, O Lord, your people;* rather it is, *Give praise, and say, "Save, O Lord, your people."* The implication is that the best way of asking for God's help is to offer praise to God. To outsiders this may seem illogical and self-deluding, but it has been proved again and again in the church's life.

Why? Because in a mysterious way praise releases energy. It makes possible visions that otherwise may not be seen. Jeremiah speaks to a people fearful and under threat, but he looks forward to a time when this people will be gathered again after being scattered, and will be strengthened again after experiencing great weakness and vulnerability. *He who scattered Israel will gather him.* The same God who brings judgement will also bring grace for recovery from the judgement.

In today's church, searching for its role in the turmoil of society, contending with vast and challenging changes in human thought, we can identify with the situation to which Jeremiah speaks. Our task is to speak to our situation as he speaks to his. He assures his people that the same God whose judgement brings hardship will eventually bring grace. *With consolations I will lead them back.* Is it possible that already, if only we can recognize it, God is offering grace for recovery and renewal? Can we deny that the comfortable Christian experience during recent centuries of Western culture has failed to judge and test our faith and church life?

In Jeremiah's vision of the return of Israel, what do the people of God return to do? To offer praise. To sing. *They shall come and sing aloud on the height of Zion, and they shall be radiant over the goodness of the Lord.* The images communicate energy. And they suggest questions that we might ask ourselves. What would our congregational life be like if we were radiant over the goodness of the Lord? What would it take for us to become like a watered garden? What would it mean for our congregation to never languish again?

Jeremiah's mind entertains images of a huge joyful party.

Young women [shall] dance ...
young men and the old shall be merry.
I will turn their mourning into joy,
... give them gladness for sorrow.

Is there not something extraordinarily contagious about this scripture? Time after time it has been shown that to praise God when there seems little reason to praise, to hope when there seems little reason to hope, to sing when there seems reason only for sobbing, is to find the strength to bring into being the very future one can now only hope for. Here is our primary vocation as contemporary Christians.

The Psalm

This psalm is exactly the kind of outburst of praise that Jeremiah is asking of his people, and it is exactly what God is asking of us in today's church. I think the most important phrase in these lines is the psalmist's assurance that God *declares his word to Jacob.* In other words, difficult times and seemingly irresolvable and divisive issues do not indicate that the relationship between God and the people of God has ceased, and they do not mean that the guidance of God has been withdrawn. The relationship is there for our claiming, and the guidance of God will be found in our faithful seeking.

Second Reading

This passage is a celebration of what it means to be Christian and, therefore, like the first reading, another rich and strong word for us today. Because the readings for this day are the same in all three years of the lectionary, I would like to refer you to my treatment of this passage in the volumes of this series for Years A and C. But in addition, I think it is helpful to recall the situation in which the Ephesians found themselves as they received this letter from St. Paul.

It is easy to read a passage like this and wish that we could live in an age of such great faith and enthusiasm. These Christians were a relatively small community in a huge cosmopolitan city where they were surrounded by all sorts of cultures and ideas and communities. In a word, they were situated very much as we are. For various reasons these men and women had been drawn to Christian faith. They shared in its sacred meal, and probably met regularly for teaching and discussion, but they were still very much in the formation stage of Christian faith. Only a generation or so since the church had begun, they were still trying to decide what it all meant. The letters of Paul helped them in their seeking. There would have been many opinions about every aspect of the new faith. There would have been many degrees of faithfulness — some people extremely committed, others just curious; some giving up and leaving, others arriving with the same mixture of motives and resolution.

But does this description not remind us of ourselves and our own time, of our Christian faith and our own church life? The similarity has become even more striking in the last four decades of this century as the position of Christians in Western culture has drastically changed. Christianity has been changing from being the faith of a culture to being one faith among many in a multiculture. Because our situation has become so like that of St. Paul and the Ephesians, we respond to these letters with a new vividness and intensity. We have to listen again to Paul's list of what God has done in Christ for us.

> *blessed us ... with every spiritual blessing ...*
> *chose us in Christ ...*
> *destined us for adoption ...*
> *[redeemed us] through his blood ...*
> *[forgiven us] our trespasses ...*
> *made known to us the mystery of his will ...*
> *marked [us] with the seal of the promised Holy Spirit.*

With such assurances we, like the Ephesians, are made strong in our seeking and faithful to our calling.

The Gospel

In the beginning was the Word. John is working on the very edge of language as he seeks to describe the significance of the arrival of Jesus in human life.

Even before time began, there existed, deep within the mystery we call God, a force or energy pulsating with creativity. Even before the creation of the universe — the Big Bang — all that was going to be was already present in this energy. It was like an unimaginably mysterious and powerful Word deep in God, waiting to be spoken.

When that energy, force, creativity, or *Word* — the term John chooses — was uttered, it exploded into being. Galaxies and worlds appeared. On one of those worlds — and perhaps on others — creatures formed that eventually began to search for something beyond themselves. Living and dying, loving and hating, suffering and rejoicing, these creatures are haunted by God even if they deny God.

The climax of creation occurs when the Word that is the source of creation becomes such a creature. *The Word became flesh and lived among us.* In that Word-in-flesh we see what John calls *glory,* and we know this glory to be a reflection of the unimaginable glory we call God.

We will never know how the Word became flesh, but we do know why. *God so loved the world that he gave his only Son, so that everyone who believes in him may not perish but have eternal life.*

Epiphany of the Lord

Isaiah 60:1–6
Psalm 72:1–7, 10–14
Ephesians 3:1–12
Matthew 2:1–12

Weavings

In all these scriptures appointed for this feast day, a great gift is being given.

First Reading. The people of God have been given the great gift of their freedom. Now they must learn how to use it in God's service.

The Psalm. The psalmist prays for the gift of justice for the newly crowned king. The hope is that, having received the gift, he will use it and so reflect the face of a God of justice.

Second Reading. Paul speaks of a gift so tremendous that it is almost unbelievable. The riches of Christ know no limits, and they are offered to all as a gift.

The Gospel. Coming from the East, surviving the dangers of Herod's court, the magi arrive at the place where the Child lies, and they offer their gifts.

Reflections

First Reading

On both sides of the Atlantic, a poet is often asked to compose a special work to mark a great point of change in a nation's history, whether it be an inauguration or a coronation. I think we can understand this passage best when we treat it as a similar kind of poem.

It looks as if the long exile in Babylon is over. But so recent is their freedom that the people cannot quite believe it, and Isaiah wants them to realize that the future shines ahead and calls them to plan and to work. His first line is almost literally a jolt, an electrifying shout: *Arise, shine; for your light has come, and the glory of the Lord has risen upon you.* There is much more involved in Isaiah's vision than the fate of a single small people. This new found freedom, this opportunity to build the future, is nothing less than the gift of God, and the significance of the gift must not be missed. The matter in hand is not Israel's glory but God's glory.

Consider for a moment a very contemporary nuance in this passage. Isaiah points out to his generation that their young people are coming home from Babylon: *Your sons shall come from far away, and your daughters shall be carried on their nurses' arms.* (I think if I were a woman listening to this passage, I would be tempted to ask Isaiah if he really meant that daughters were any less capable of walking home than sons!) All levity aside — the image of young people returning to build the future reminds us of an appalling situation in our own time. Even when every sign of the economy is indicating prosperity and growth — *the abundance of the sea ... brought to you ... the wealth of nations shall come to you* — we still show no signs of being able to build a world where millions of young people will be employed!

If this passage were to be used for a homily at Epiphany, I would suggest that we see a parallel between the people of God long ago being given back not only their land and their city but also their sense of identity, and the Christian people of God being given the gift of our Lord. Just as Isaiah's listeners needed to understand what their gift meant — new hope and new possibilities — so we have to realize what the timeless gift of our Lord means in hope and spiritual possibilities for us.

The Psalm

Whenever a new head of state takes office, we regard it as quite normal to hear him or her make certain promises. They will be phrased differently, depending on the person assuming high office or the conditions of the country at the time. But the promises will always have certain constant themes. The new ruler will promise to be a person of integrity, to be concerned for all the people rather than some element within the society. In a word, his or her promise will be to be a good head of state.

There may be another element in these promises. Often new rulers will acknowledge that they stand before a higher court than human society. They take their authority from God. When we ask where these customs come from, we turn to the Bible. This psalm is one of the most explicit statements about the source of authority in society. *Give the king your justice, O God.* But why this prayerful request? For one purpose — that the king may *rule your people righteously and ... with justice.*

The people are not the possession of the ruler. The people, says the psalmist, are *your [God's] people.* Millennia before we ever hear language such as "having a preferential option for the poor," this psalm emphasizes the cause of *the needy ... the poor.* Only if this cause is pursued will the society be one where *the righteous flourish;* and *there shall be an abundance of peace.* The moral integrity of such a society will make it a blessing among other nations.

Christians look for righteousness and peace within the ministry of our Lord. We see the vision in his words again and again. No earthly society can ever rise completely to his moral challenge, but our never-ending hope that these values will not disappear from public life is based solidly on the light that streams at this season from the Christ who has accepted the poverty of coming among us.

Second Reading

It is easy to miss the immensity of the concept Paul is trying to convey to his readers in this passage. He wisely takes a few lines building up to it. By using the word *mystery* no less than three times, he draws our attention and curiosity. It is impossible not to ask, "What is this mystery?" Like a good story teller, he suggests that it has been hidden from others but is now about to be revealed to his listeners: *In former generations this mystery was not made known ... it has now been revealed.*

When the mystery was revealed, it was indeed astounding for those who heard it. For Jewish followers of Jesus, it could also have been deeply troubling. The mystery was that the new faith in Jesus as Christ knew no limits whatsoever! It was for the world — nothing less. As it is true that *God [has] created all things,* so it is now true that faith in the person known as God's son is offered and is accessible to all men and women. I am inclined to think that this passage addresses us especially these days in an increasingly multicultural world. Perhaps it is more true to say, an increasingly multicultural *society.* After all, the world has always been multicultural! We just did not realize this fully; and if we did, it was through visiting other cultures but returning home to the known and familiar.

More and more we talk about possible future relationships between the great religions now mingling in our streets. Yet before we talk about this, we need perhaps to remind ourselves that, within the many races sharing our local shopping centre, there are also many Christians! We can sympathize with the difficulty that the Jewish people of Paul's time may have had in realizing that Christ knows no boundaries of race. Paul speaks of *the wisdom of God in its rich variety.* The evidence for this is all around us.

Of this gospel I have become a servant, says Paul. The question we need to ask is whether we ourselves have become a servant of this gospel, whether we are prepared to accept this great mystery of the Christ of no boundaries.

The Gospel

After Jesus was born ... wise men from the East came to Jerusalem. Who they were, what they did in their society, where precisely they came from, why they made this journey — none of these questions has ever been answered. Guesses and probabilities abound, but no more. Because we know so little about them, these travellers have become figures of high and endless romance. One of the most haunting expressions of their journey is "The Coming of the Magi" by T.S. Eliot, and it might possibly be useful for this Sunday, perhaps read by more than one voice.

Everything about their journey provides rich material for reflecting on our own Christian journey. We begin at the first parallel between their lives and ours — they journeyed, as do we. Does this make us wise? It would seem so, if travelling means that we experience constant change in our lives, and that we are continually deepening and maturing. Refusal to do this kind of inner travelling can result in a shallow and limited spiritual life.

We observed his star at its rising. This season of the church year is trying to get us to do precisely this — to become aware of Christ as a kind of star, a shining light that calls us to travel towards it.

In the time of King Herod. The old king signifies every-thing that is the enemy of this journey. He wishes that the jour-ney had never taken place, and he is determined to end it or to use it for his own purposes. In our own spiritual journey there are danger points. Herod turns up in many disguises. Many things conspire to halt or side-track our journey towards our Lord. Most of them are deceptively ordinary things — busi-ness, weariness, depression, anxiety, cynicism.

When they had heard the king, they set out. For some rea-son I like the sound of *they set out.* There is a hint that they knew they had been side-tracked. We too need to realize when we have been distracted from our journey, when we have left the main highway for attractive detours that end in *cul de sacs!* Then we need to recoup, turn around, and once again *set out,* realizing that, although we may have chosen another direction, our "star" did not, and that we need to look for it again.

On entering the house ... they knelt down and ... offered him gifts. This scene is engraved on the minds of most people from innumerable children's pageants! But the same scene speaks to the depths of our human experience. It is absolutely neces-sary in life to have something for which we are prepared to search, to risk, and when we find it, to bow down and offer our gifts. If that something is worthy and good and pure, then we are indeed rich. We are, one might say, kings.

For a Christian, the ultimate reality to journey towards and to search for, is our Lord Jesus Christ. If and when we find this presence in our lives, our instinct is to bow down and offer the best that is in us, the gifts we bring. It is easy to forget that the gifts we have were given by God in the first place. When we lay them before Jesus as our Lord, we are merely returning what we have been given. But even so, we grow in the giving. For in the enterprise of giving, we somehow touch the mystery of that greatest of journeys — the journey of God.

Baptism of the Lord

Genesis 1:1–5
Psalm 29
Acts 19:1–7
Mark 1:4–11

Weavings

There is about all these scriptures a quality of new beginning, of sunrise, of morning, of new day.

In the first reading we are present at the morning of creation, watching the universe blazing in its first light. In the psalm it is almost as if we are watching as God walks onto the stage of creation in power and majesty. In the second reading we watch as a group of people realize that there is far more to the gospel message than they thought. This realization sweeps over them and changes them. In the gospel we see John the Baptist appear like a sudden blaze of light among his people, speaking of a new day and calling them to new commitment. Later in the passage Jesus himself appears, and for us, the ultimate light is kindled.

Reflections

First Reading

This Sunday the first reading and the gospel are very much interwoven. Here are five links between the two passages.

1. *In the beginning when God created.* That this passage is given to us along with Mark's description of our Lord's baptism tells us that, for a Christian, the baptism of our Lord is in itself a kind of new creation.

2. As we read in this passage that a wind from God swept over the face of the waters, we are being pointed to the presence of the Holy Spirit, the breath or wind of God, at Jesus' baptism.

3. Again, when in this passage God says, *Let there be light,* we realize that our Lord's baptism brings into human experience a new source of light.

4. The writer of Genesis tells us how God saw that the light was good. We are about to hear these words echoed as Jesus comes from the waters of baptism and the voice of God expresses approval.

5. Just as in the first reading, we are present at the first day; so as we watch Jesus accept baptism, we are sharing the first day of his public ministry.

These five connections suggest questions for meditation.

• What is it that faith in Jesus Christ creates within my life?

- In what ways is my faith in the Holy Spirit of God a force that motivates or drives my thinking and acting?

- In what ways is belief in Christ as my Lord a guiding light in my life?

What might it mean for me to experience a sense of the approval of God, a sense that God regards some decision or action of mine as good? For example, if I become convinced that a certain course of action has God's approval and reflects God's will for my life so far as I can discern that will, how does this affect me? Does it give me courage to go ahead? Does it strengthen my resolve to overcome obstacles? Does it relax tensions I may have had during the struggle to discern God's will?

In what way have some of my experiences had the quality of being the first day of a new stage in my life? Consider some important decisions — a decision to marry, to change jobs, to take a great risk, to settle in a distant place, to hold my newborn child. On such days of decision or change or new direction, did my faith in Christ have any significant influence?

The Psalm

The presence of God is overwhelming in these verses. Nothing else matters; nothing else is of any importance. Notice how frequently the word *Lord* occurs — eighteen in my count.

When I read these verses, I have the feeling of someone caught outside in a storm — the driving wind, the breaking and crashing branches, the drumming of heavy rain, the searing lightning, the roar of thunder.

My feelings in all this? At first, fear and the instinct to preserve myself. Then, a wild almost savage exhilaration — as if I and the storm had become one, and we were both servants of the Lord of the storm. I find myself shouting "Glory!" into the wind and the torrential rain. There is a sense of self-abandonment. I am intoxicated by the might and glory of God. In all this I am nothing, yet I am God's creature.

All of this echoes what the writer of Genesis is communicating and, later, what the gospel writer is telling us. Both writers are trying to describe events utterly beyond their capacity to comprehend — the creation itself, and the entry of God in human flesh into the arena of public life. Writer and readers alike can do nothing more than surrender to the majesty and the wonder of what is taking place. If we say anything in response, it can only be a silent or whispered "Glory!"

Second Reading

Apollos is an intriguing figure, if only because we know enough about him to want to know more. He was a gifted and energetic Jew from Alexandria, who had been so excited and captivated by the words and work of John the Baptist that he began to travel across the Mediterranean world with a group of companions, just as Paul did with his companions. Apollos knew his Hebrew scriptures well, and he was aware of the story being told about Jesus, but he had not moved to the acceptance of Jesus as Lord. He had succeeded in forming some communities, even in large sophisticated centres such as Ephesus, where he had called people to a baptism like John's, but he had taken them no further in the faith.

One wonders what Paul's reaction was when he first arrived in Ephesus, following Apollos's time there. Here was a community versed in their own scriptures, aware of the work of John, aware to a certain extent of Jesus, but not yet a conscious and intentional Christian community.

I see many contemporary congregations in something of the same situation. There is a passing knowledge of the scriptures, the sacraments are celebrated, Jesus is a familiar figure in public worship. But the congregation must journey a thousand miles before they will realize the significance of our Lord and his claims upon those who would follow him. If Paul could travel in time and join us in our congregational life, what would he say?

I suspect that Paul, being the great missionary that he was, took the Ephesus situation in his stride and immediately thought of ways to use it. He first ascertains where in faith these men and women are — he asks about their awareness of the Holy Spirit. He finds that they have none because Apollos had not mentioned the Holy Spirit. Paul does not ridicule or condemn but takes a step back — he asks about baptism. Then comes the heart of the matter. He knows what to do. Paul builds a bridge from John to Jesus and leads these people across it. In so doing, he gives a gift to every leader of a Christian congregation or group, a classic lesson in meeting people where they are, in order to teach and lead them to Christian commitment. He opens their hearts to the gifts of the Holy Spirit.

The Gospel

John the baptizer appeared in the wilderness, proclaiming a baptism of repentance for the forgiveness of sins. In this packed opening sentence, Mark tells us a great deal very quickly and succinctly. Notice the shocking quality of John's appearing. One day he is not there; the next day he is. Notice that John comes proclaiming. There is nothing apologetic about his approach. Proclamation demands attention and reaction — negative or positive. Notice, too, how the idea of baptism is mentioned twice. To say Yes to such an invitation is a very significant decision. It commits one to act very publicly and to reveal a great deal about one's private life. Acknowledging that we wish to repent of what we have said or done, and to do so publicly in order to receive forgiveness of sins, is all very serious. There is little wonder that John made such a powerful impression on his society, either incurring its anger and resentment or attracting a faithful following.

Those who listened to John may have been intrigued by the obvious humility of the man. He was quite clearly not trying to build some personal empire. He saw himself as preparing for someone much more significant than himself. There was an undoubted attractiveness in the way that he referred to this coming figure, insisting that he was unworthy to stoop down and untie the thong of his sandals.

We are seeing here a pattern for Christian leadership of any kind. Whatever situation of leadership we may be in, either within the life of the church or in our own professional life, we find that people are drawn to one who is not merely building a personal empire, small or large, but is genuinely committed to the task in hand and to the lives of those with whom the task is being done. I wonder if this was one of the traits in John that so endeared him to our Lord.

When we hear John say, *I have baptized you with water; but he will baptize you with the Holy Spirit,* it is easy to miss the deep humility in the statement. John recognizes his limitations. He can carry the task so far; then he must hand over to one who can carry it further. This too is a lesson for our lives.

Jesus came from Nazareth of Galilee and was baptized by John in the Jordan. If we turn for a moment from Mark's description to Matthew's (3:14), we see yet another attractive trait in the character of John. When Jesus offers himself for baptism, John says, *I need to be baptized by you, and do you come to me?* This generous gesture proves without doubt that John has been genuine in his claim to be nothing more than an ambassador for a greater one to come. That he should say these words publicly makes them even more self-effacing. Here is John, surrounded by a vast following that hangs on his words, giving first place without a moment's hesitation to this stranger who has just arrived in the area.

We leave John and turn our attention to our Lord. To seek this baptism as John gave it, to seek it publicly on the terms that John offered it, was to radically reveal oneself to others. The mere fact that one entered the water clad only with minimal clothing was itself a symbol of this self-revealing. Yet our Lord does this.

If our Lord accepts the grace of baptism, how much more is it true that I should be aware of what my baptism means for me. If our Lord acknowledges that baptism is for the forgiveness of sins, how incalculably more do I need to be thankful for God's unconditional acceptance of my life, pathetic and wretched as it is beside that of our Lord.

Mark tells us that a voice came from heaven: *You are my Son, the Beloved; with you I am well pleased.* As Christians, you and I possess the assurance that these words are addressed to us, undeserving of them as we are. "You are my Son." "You are my daughter." We need constant reminding that the reason we have this assurance of God's unconditional and entirely undeserved acceptance is that in his baptism our Lord identified with our human condition, accepted the terrible baptism of death at our hands, and finally offered us the hope and grace of his resurrected life.

Second Sunday after the Epiphany: Proper 2

1 Samuel 3:1–10, (11–20)
Psalm 139:1–5, 13–18
I Corinthians 6:12–20
John 1:43–51

Weavings

The common theme of these passages is being called to serve. In the first reading the boy Samuel is called by God to future responsibility. In the psalm the poet is called to acknowledge the greatness of God's creative powers, particularly in the formation of the poet's own humanity. In the second reading Paul calls the self-indulgent Corinthian community to moral and disciplined living. In the gospel we hear our Lord calling disciples, who in turn call others to the same allegiance.

Reflections

First Reading

The times in which this great story is set were irreligious. *The word of the Lord was rare in those days: visions were not widespread.* Even the vivid image of the lamp — *the lamp of God had not yet gone out* — suggests the flickering state of the country's spirit.

The main character in the story is the old priest Eli, now beginning to withdraw from his heavy responsibilities. On the other hand, young Samuel is full of a sense of the importance of his new duties. One is ending, the other is beginning. One is the past, the other the future.

The reiteration of God's call to the boy is beautifully and vividly told. At the third call something happens that says a great deal about the old man. Old age finally tumbles to the fact that God is calling youth.

Old age often finds it easier to affirm the presence and action of God in the past rather than the present. This is, of course, a generalization. We all know wonderful exceptions, but they tend nevertheless to prove the rule. Here Eli shows his greatness, not only by recognizing the entry of God into this moment, but also by showing no jealousy about the obvious course of events — in effect, his own displacement.

Again, in Eli's encounter with Samuel in the morning, we see the quality of this great human being. We know from elsewhere in scripture, as well as from this passage, that Eli has fallen on sad times. He has allowed himself to become obese. His sons have shamed and discredited him, and his name, and his high office. He must feel a terrible sense of personal failure. The last thing Samuel wants to do is to report to Eli the terrible things he now knows. But Eli insists, and when at last he hears what the Lord has said to Samuel, we again see the old man's greatness. There is not a hint of resentment, not a whisper of self-pity or self-justification.

I see a human being who even in his decline shows what once made him great, an elderly person who is open to the action of God in the present moment, who is totally devoid of

jealousy and rancour, and who courageously accepts the consequences without flinching. Such an example must have helped
to form the future greatness of Samuel.

The Psalm

Lord, you have searched me and known me. If we find it possible to say this line without some sense of nakedness, we are
not really taking in what it means. Think of the threat of being
searched, or the threat of being completely and utterly known
to someone else. There is no place to hide. Yet the psalmist is
telling us that God has already searched and known us. Before
God we are naked. No action I do, no thought I have, no word
I utter, but *[God] is acquainted with all my ways.*

However, this knowledge is bearable because I am a creature of God's own making. I have no need to hide, to pretend,
to mask, to conceal, because all is already known. *My body was
not hidden from you.*

The good news is that before God I can be totally honest
and totally relaxed about who and what I am. My response then,
far from being one of shame or fear or resentment at this all-
seeing eye of God, is one of praise. *I will thank you because I
am marvellously made.* The fact that I have been formed by
God overcomes whatever shame and shortcomings I may be
only too painfully aware of. I can respond to God's call to service precisely because this is what God has formed me to do.

Second Reading

All things are lawful for me, but not all things are beneficial.
Once again we need to remind ourselves of the kind of society
that Paul is writing to. There was a strong tendency in the Mediterranean world of that time to take refuge in the satisfaction of
appetite, whether for food, sex, clothes, drink, or luxury goods

of various kinds. We hear Paul calling for a lifestyle in which self-discipline curbs self-indulgence and inhibits the cravings of appetite.

He continues by mentioning the prevalence of promiscuous sex in the culture and — we have to assume — in the community itself. Perhaps it is important to point out that Paul is not condemning human sexuality as in any way unworthy. His concern is not with sexuality but with promiscuity, especially prostitution. Our culture, too, needs to hear what he says. The sexual act can never be merely physical. Since it involves two human beings, it involves them at levels of the mind and the spirit. We can no more avoid this involvement than we can climb out of our skins. We are both spiritual and physical beings.

Paul calls attention to our human wholeness in the form of a question: *Do you not know that your body is a temple of the Holy Spirit within you?* By linking the body to the spirit, and the spirit to its ultimate source, the Spirit of God, he points out that our humanity has a value and a meaning far beyond its human value. Ultimately our humanity is sacred — a sacred gift. Notice how Paul's statement, *You are not your own,* challenges much that our present culture claims for individual autonomy and the ever-present claim to "my rights."

The Gospel

My guess is that Jesus has returned from his time in the desert. He has wrestled with the different options for his future — what elsewhere in the gospels is called his temptations or his testing. He has decided that his future course of action will entail the forming of a core community. Now we see this process beginning. *He found Philip and said to him, "Follow me."*

Soon comes a most significant statement, easily missed because it sounds so straightforward and natural: *Philip found*

Nathanael. Here in this gospel moment we hear someone (Philip) witnessing to his relationship with Jesus by telling someone else (Nathanael) what it means to him, thereby inviting the other into a similar relationship. The future of the Christian church in our Western culture may depend on a return to this simple — but to many, daunting — ministry of all Christians. We need to learn the art of inviting others to relationship with our Lord, with Christian faith, and with its community.

Notice how Philip presents the invitation to Nathanael in terms that the latter can identify with. Maybe the two friends have often discussed the tantalizing and mysterious figure in the prophetic writings — he who is supposed to come some day. Philip finds Nathanael and in effect says, "You know that figure we've often talked about? I think he has come! In fact, I have met him, and I think you should, too."

Similarly, we must find the appropriate entry points into another's spiritual space. Maybe there is a search for meaning in life. Maybe there is a sense of great loss. Our task is to speak of our Lord in such a way that he in turn speaks to the human spirit in its deepest need, as Philip spoke to Nathanael's need.

Nathanael's grumpy response has become legendary, but it did not put Philip off. Enthusiasm and warmth won the day. We need to note this. It is easy to think that Christian evangelism calls for the ability to answer questions with some officially correct answers. But the honest enthusiasm of a friend whom we like and trust has the greatest chance of drawing us. When someone who knows me well says, "You simply must see such and such a show" or "You simply must read such and such a book," I do not ask a dozen precise questions as to why. I am intrigued and drawn to the possibility on the basis of the relationship. We cannot afford to neglect this great truth in today's church life.

The rest of this passage seems a kind of bantering between Jesus and Nathanael. Sensing that Nathanael is here only grudgingly, our Lord is especially warm and affirming. I see him putting his hands on Nathanael's shoulders when he says heartily, *Here is truly an Israelite in whom there is no deceit!* When Nathanael receives these words in a stolid and literal way, asking, *Where did you get to know me?* Jesus pushes the whimsy even further. Perhaps a wink to Philip goes with, *I saw you under the fig tree before Philip called you.* Now Nathanael begins to thaw. I see a sudden grin as he responds at last to Jesus' mood. As soon as our Lord knows that he has broken through Nathanael's defences, he moves to seriousness.

Do you believe ...? You will see greater things.... What Jesus is saying to Nathanael is a truth that we discover in many ways. When we say an initial Yes to something or to somebody, we may be initiating a significant action or relationship. Only long after do we realize that we really had no idea of what we were saying our Yes to, no idea of how deep a love would grow, how intense a loyalty would develop, how involved a commitment would become, or how costly. Just as our Lord points out to Nathanael that one day he will realize what began at this moment of meeting, so eventually we discover the immense significance of our early Yes.

Third Sunday after the Epiphany: Proper 3

Jonah 3:1–5, 10
Psalm 62:5–12
I Corinthians 7:29–31
Mark 1:14–20

Weavings

I hear these scriptures saying something like this: there come times when something or someone tells us that everything is going to be changed utterly. Things will never be the same again. When this happens, a response is demanded of us. What is that response going to be?

I hear this proclamation of change in the first reading when Jonah speaks to Nineveh, in the second reading when Paul speaks to the Corinthian community, and in the gospel when Jesus addresses the Galilee of his time and his future disciples in particular. Through all of this the psalmist sings of the God who is the only constant in all change.

Reflections

First Reading

First let us consider the story of Jonah, a wonderful story, full of irony and humour. It fits with the overall theme of the Epiphany season because it is about journeying, questing, searching — even if in Jonah's case the questing is done most grudgingly. It is about discovery, including for Jonah a great deal of self-discovery, especially about the nature of the God who will not leave him alone to his own selfish life. Our own lives, too, are full of self-discovery and discovery about the nature of the God who prods and pushes us to be much more than we want to be.

God wants Jonah to go to the great city of Nineveh and warn its inhabitants of the consequences of their own wickedness. Jonah is adamant that he does not want to go. He does not care about the people of Nineveh whom God wishes to save. Every effort that Jonah makes to evade God's call is thwarted. But he eventually ends up, much against his wishes, just outside the very city that God wants him to address.

In the short passage set for today, Jonah has arrived at Nineveh. He goes into its streets and shouts out what God wants him to say. Through Jonah, God warns these people that, if they do not change their evil ways, they are courting disaster. Jonah is so angry about being involved in God's scheme that he not only believes the people of Nineveh will ignore him but even wishes for their destruction. Yet to his utter astonishment the people both listen and respond — they change their ways! Such is the power of God's word, even in a reluctant but faithful servant.

The Psalm

The first line of this psalm is a beautiful and valuable invitation to quiet reflection. I have found it helpful when said quietly or silently at intervals. At these times I try to do just what the words say: to wait in silence for God.

This simple use of even a short period of time is extremely difficult in our culture. Everything conspires against it, unless we make a great effort to shut ourselves away where there can be no interruption. Since we cannot always manage to be isolated, we have to develop a way of waiting in silence for God when we are still surrounded by demands, interruptions, and claims on our time and attention. But even a few minutes grasped from the ongoing pulse of living is sufficient, a few minutes of silencing the phone, darkening the computer screen, being alone.

Having said these lines of this psalm, perhaps I reflect silently on God asking what my life is grounded on. What is it that makes it possible for me to stand firmly in life? In what sense is God my rock, my salvation, my refuge, my fortress? Who are the people given me by God, on whom I can rely and draw for support?

As in last week's psalm, I am asked to hide nothing but, rather, to pour out my heart before God. When I do so, I discover that I am both judged and loved. Knowing that the latter is true makes the former bearable. *I heard ... that power belongs to God, [and] steadfast love.*

Second Reading

We have to get under the language of the time to hear the timeless truth in what Paul is saying. Immediately before the passage set for today are words about wives — words that seem dismissive and male chauvinist. In Paul's culture they would not have sounded so. Instead of rejecting what he writes, I suggest we hear Paul as talking about relationships in general and saying something like this. Relationships, feelings, personal experiences, possessions, business affairs are all to be viewed through a certain lens. This lens is the certainty that the whole of human life and human experience is about to be transformed into a new reality whose form we cannot predict. *The present form of this world is passing away.*

It is obvious that Paul expects this vast transformation at any time. We could argue that, as Christians, we should live as if this great transformation may occur at any moment, but the reality is that we do not and, I would suggest, cannot. As the years went by, Christians learned that it was much healthier to leave the time of any such transformation to God and, meanwhile, to live in the personal and public realm with all the grace and integrity that one could.

But there still remains a truth we can take from this passage. It is not a truth any of us wishes to hear. Nothing in life, however lovely or precious it may be — our dearest loves, our greatest achievements, our most precious possessions — nothing is itself ultimate. All exist within time and are therefore transitory. Lord Byron once wrote, "There's not a joy the world can give like that it takes away." But Paul is saying something deeper. He is telling us that all these things exist in the flow of time and change but that they find their ultimacy only in God. And because all aspects of our lives, from our deepest personal relationships to our professional strivings and achievements, exist in a flow of change, we must be constantly aware of the necessity for renewal.

The Gospel

Our Lord himself takes up the theme of change and renewal. In being called to begin his public ministry he has himself felt great turmoil at the most personal level. He is convinced that some great change must be envisioned. His name for this change is the kingdom of God. It is the vision of a changed society and changed people. This vision has obviously taken hold of Jesus and charged him with a sense of mission. In this passage we see him setting out to infect others with his enthusiasm.

We can almost hear the passion and excitement in Jesus' voice as he turns to the men who were to become his closest friends and says with intensity, *Follow me and I will make you fish for people.* In other words, "I will transform your lives. What you do, who you are, where you go, what you hope for — all will change if you catch this vision I offer you."

Their response — *Immediately they left their nets and followed him* — shows that they were swept into Jesus' passionate intensity. As we watch them walking away from us down that long-ago beach, we have to decide what all this means for us who hear this passage.

Consider for a moment who we are. Just as the fishermen were probably devout synagogue-attending Jews, so most of us are people who have grown up in Christian faith, or have recently discovered it, or are still searching towards it. No matter what stage we are at, this gospel passage is telling us that our Lord constantly comes to our present state and calls us to move to something greater, to journey with him farther and deeper, to be always open to possibility and always prepared to respond.

For instance, we can easily assume that the life of a congregation is an end in itself. Every congregation faces endless tasks to keep its own life going. Yet our Lord comes to us in our day, just as he came to those men long ago, and calls us to *fish for people*, whether those people were once part of the community and have been somehow lost to it, or whether they are in the greater community in which the church and the congregation are set.

Our Lord comes and says, "Do not forget my vision of the kingdom of God." Where did Jesus get that vision? From the scriptures in which he was brought up. And what has that kingdom always meant? Justice. That single word is used again and again in scripture to name God's will and longing for human society.

When our Lord comes into the life of a congregation reminding us of his vision of the kingdom of God, he is asking us to act in the surrounding society to make it a little more just and caring. And if responding to this call of our Lord means that some changes have to be made in the way we live as a congregation, then this is exactly what our Lord calls us to, just as God called Jonah to change in a way he found costly, and just as Paul points out that every aspect of our lives, personal and corporate, is lived in the context of constant and costly change.

But as the psalmist has already reminded us, God is constant amid change. This mysterious relationship between change and changelessness has been beautifully expressed by Thomas Cranmer, who was Archbishop of Canterbury at a most turbulent time in his country's history. That turbulence cost Cranmer his life. In one prayer that he wrote and inserted in our *Book of Common Prayer*, he prays "that we may so pass through things temporal that we finally lose not the things eternal," and in another that "among the sundry and manifold changes of the world, our hearts may surely there be fixed where true joys are to be found." We can make these prayers our own as we move through the vast and hurtling transitions of our own time.

Fourth Sunday after the Epiphany: Proper 4

Deuteronomy 18:15–20
Psalm 111
1 Corinthians 8:1–13
Mark 1:21–28

Weavings

Throughout these passages there is a note of sternness. God makes stern demands on those who would claim to be faithful.

In the first reading the people's request for a prophet is shown to have very real and salutary consequences. In the second reading Paul draws a clear line between other religious systems in the culture and the new faith in Christ. In the gospel passage, Jesus' strong response to the challenge from the crowd is given without the least compromise. The psalmist, while praising God, is aware that intimacy with God must always be mingled with awe.

Reflections

First Reading

The book of Deuteronomy was found while some repairs were being made on the temple, at a time when standards had slipped very badly in Israel's life. It commanded immense respect. Very beautifully written, it offered a high moral challenge and issued a call to faithfulness that challenged all those who read it or heard it read aloud.

Today's passage is typical of the book. The writer is addressing the people of God on the authority of Moses, the giant of their past, who brought them through the wilderness experience. They were camped in the general region of Sinai, an active volcano of awe-inspiring grandeur in those days. Moses had chosen this place to present the moral demands of God in the form of the ten commandments. If you want to recall the description of this moment, turn back to Deuteronomy 5:22–27. To read this passage is to be helped in making sense of today's scripture.

Moses had come out of the smoke and thunder of Sinai with the commandments. The people were awestruck. They knew that he had risked death to do this. That he should return at all was astonishing. They had no wish to do what he had done and would do again on their behalf. *Go near, you yourself, and hear all that the Lord our God will say. Then tell us everything that the Lord our God tells you, and we will listen and do it.*

Now we come back to this Sunday's passage. The people are being reminded of the way in which they had given Moses the responsibility of standing between themselves and the fearful presence of God. Now, at this later stage in their history, they are being told that there will again be those who stand between them and God. These people will be known as prophets, and they will have great moral standing in the life of the people. They will speak responsibly and, therefore, with authority. If these prophets in any way abuse their great privilege, they will have to answer for it. The penalty is nothing less than death. But also, those who refuse to listen and obey when a prophet speaks are to be held accountable.

Consider the infinite distance between our world and this world of the Bible. The ancient Israelites lived in a society where the reality of God was taken utterly for granted. We live in a society where many doubt this reality and some contemptuously dismiss it.

The Israelites took absolutely for granted that they lived in a moral world. This is not to say that they always acted morally, but even when they did not, they were fully aware that they were trespassing against a traditionally established code. Our culture strongly doubts that there is such a thing as a moral law, apart from our varied and shifting perceptions of what may or may not be moral.

The Israelites lived in a world of hierarchical authorities, among whom were the prophets. We live in a society where all authorities are questioned and challenged, and where all hierarchy is seen as inherently oppressive and, therefore, unacceptable. Today's reading brings into sharp focus the intense cultural disparity between the world of the Bible and the world where we, who now read the Bible, live.

The Psalm

The great philosopher Emmanuel Kant contended that, although our human knowledge would always be no more than perceptions of the truth, there would always be two things we could look to as the ground of reality: "the silent stars above and the moral law within" — a lovely phrase. He may well have been echoing two equally lovely lines from Dante's *Divine Comedy:* "The love that rules my heart and mind is the love that moves the sun and stars." Both these great minds are indebted to the psalmist for their insights.

All through the psalms God is present as the ground of all being. Today's psalm is a hymn of praise: *Great are the deeds of the Lord!* The defining marks of God are majesty, splendour, and righteousness.

Then, as often in the psalms, there is the counter theme. The same God who is praised for his power is praised also for his gentleness: *the Lord is gracious and full of compassion.* This creator of galaxies also *gives food to those who fear him.* He is a God of *faithfulness and justice.* We can see that these same attributes should be found in our own humanity.

Through these two themes runs a third. We hear it in such phrases as *all his commandments are sure ... he commanded his covenant for ever.* Here is assurance that God is no transient power; God can be depended on.

Before such a holy and awesome God there is only one response for the psalmist: *The fear of the Lord is the beginning of wisdom.*

Second Reading

Now concerning food sacrificed to idols. Although the particular issue in this passage no longer touches our lives, we nevertheless encounter it in other forms.

In the days when this letter was written, meat used in religious sacrificial rites would usually turn up in the butchers' stalls at the market place, where people would buy it like any other meat. Christians, however, saw a serious problem with this. Since such meat had been dedicated to a pagan god, it must be unsuitable for a Christian to buy and eat.

Paul deals with the situation gently and thoughtfully. He points out that, for a Christian, the gods to whom this meat has been dedicated are not real. Only God is God. Therefore, the meat is like any other meat, nothing more or less, and it is perfectly acceptable to eat. *We are no worse off if we do not eat, and no better off if we do.*

We see here a very early example of the moral dilemmas that face Christians in any society, in some more than others. In the movie *Chariots of Fire* there is a scene where Eric Liddell, competing in the Olympics for England, refuses to run in the preliminary heats on Sunday. This means that he will be excluded from the final race. It is the nineteen-twenties. Liddell is a Christian who sincerely believes that to run on Sunday will desecrate the Lord's Day. We today may agree or disagree. I offer the incident as an issue of the kind that early Christians faced.

In one sense this passage from Paul's writing may seem far away from us, but in other ways it is very near to our experience. Today there are many Christian men and women who must work on Sundays because their union or their corporation or the pressing demands of the job require it. There are also many who feel they must seek social change because their conscience or a Charter of Rights or a contemporary Christian view demands it. Such beliefs and actions may conflict with centuries of traditional understanding.

Paul is very thoughtful and sensitive in his warnings to those who decide to ignore the source of the meat they purchase. There are some who can understand what he is saying about the unreality of the old pagan gods, but there are many for whom the pagan gods have been so much and for so long part of their lives that they cannot conceive of them as other than real. For such a person, the sight of others — especially leaders — in the Christian community eating such meat would be deeply troubling. To trouble them in this way is to be avoided if possible. To avoid offending it may be necessary to deprive oneself of a pleasure.

Paul is pointing out that all our actions can have consequences of which we are totally oblivious. We can affect other lives in ways we never dream of.

The Gospel

They went to Capernaum ... [Jesus] entered the synagogue and taught. It is interesting that Jesus is able to teach in the synagogue in Capernaum. There would have been little chance of his being invited to preach in the south since, from the point of view of Jerusalem, Galilee tended to be dismissed as liberal and, therefore, dangerous.

We can assume that our Lord's presence was magnetic and intriguing to those who encountered him in a public context. He spoke with an extraordinary authority that people could not ignore. Most were drawn, even mesmerized. But very often a charismatic and compelling speaker will engender responses other than receptive. Some people become angry and some deeply emotional. Some read into the words of the speaker what they themselves wish to hear.

In this particular crowd there is a deeply disturbed person. The moment Jesus hears the harsh, angry voice, he realizes that the situation has to be dealt with swiftly and decisively. I cannot help but hear our Lord's words, *Be silent, and come out of him,* as spoken with ringing command. Each syllable is bitten out, sharp-edged and precise. The command has an immediate effect on the person who erupted a moment before. And it probably chills the crowd into an awed silence, as they watch Jesus behaving with absolute sureness and command.

Here we glimpse a quality of our Lord that we tend seldom to look for. Seeing our Lord act with an authority immediately recognizable by those around him helps us to understand the subsequent order of events in the gospels. The kind and gentle Jesus of much sentimental Christian imaging, far from incurring the fear and wrath of the powers of his day, would never have drawn about him men and women who became ready to die for him. A pleasant demeanour, a capacity for telling stories, a caring disposition, even a certain gift for healing, might have won for our Lord the attention of the curious and some degree of public affection. But these attributes alone would never have exploded into the deadly cocktail of hatred and political maneouvering that eventually brought him to the cross. For me the value of this passage is the glimpse it gives us of the immense natural authority that was clearly present in Jesus' words and actions.

Fifth Sunday after the Epiphany: Proper 5

Isaiah 40:21–31
Psalm 147:1–12, 21c
1 Corinthians 9:16–23
Mark 1:29–39

Weavings

Divine energy infuses today's readings. In the first reading Isaiah points to God as the source of the unimaginable energy that brought creation into being and sustains life. The psalmist points to God as creator and sustainer of all. In the second reading Paul's love for the good news of his Lord fills him with focused energy to preach this same good news. In the gospel we see an ailing woman given renewed energy and life by the touch of our Lord; then we see this energy flowing to countless others who are brought for healing.

Reflections

First Reading

William Blake once spoke of holding "infinity in the palm of the hand and eternity in an hour." Isaiah was a person who could always see the great in the small. Throughout the entire

Bible he is not surpassed in the majesty of his language or the sheer scale of his lyrical prose.

I find myself responding to the questions he hurls almost fiercely at those listening to him. I hear myself being directly addressed and challenged never to take the greatness of God for granted. *Have you not known? Have you not heard? Has it not been told you from the beginning? Have you not understood ...?* We say that we know the greatness of God, but very often it is only a concept in our minds — dry, one dimensional, dispassionately held. All of us have heard countless times that God is great, is creator of all, is this and that and the other, but the words have become so familiar that we turn away from them unmoved. Isaiah knows that this is true also of those listening to him; so he sets out to explode their minds with the majesty of his language.

Let the name of God sound like the booming of a great bell.

[God] sits above the circle of the earth.
[To God] the inhabitants of the earth are like grasshoppers.
[God] stretches out the heavens like a curtain.
[God] spreads the heavens like a tent to live in.

It is easy to miss the power of the tent image. One would expect Isaiah to search for a term that would describe a massive building — perhaps the word *temple*. Instead he points to a God for whom even the heavens are no more than a tent, a place for God to rest before even greater journeying.

Isaiah turns from nature to history. God is above and beyond all earthly powers. God makes the rulers of the earth as nothing. Remember the circumstances in which Isaiah is speaking. His people have just witnessed the passing of an empire that dragged them into exile and destroyed their country. Another empire is rising, one that is so far friendly to them, even allowing them to return to Jerusalem if they wish. Isaiah is trying to get his people to see that even the greatest human systems and structures are less than God. No way of life is God, no political philosophy is God, no one view of history is God, no one view of society is God. Only God is God. All of this is desperately important for us to hear today, living as we do in economic and cultural systems far greater than anyone in Isaiah's day could imagine.

Isaiah detects some grumbling and resentment. He confronts them. *Why do you say ... my right is disregarded by my God?* The grim conditions they faced, as they journeyed back to find a ruined city waiting for them to rebuild, may have induced an understandable despondency. Into this despondency Isaiah brings a portrait of God as the source of all energy — spiritual and physical. God *gives power to the faint* and strengthens the powerless. Suddenly those listening hear something they will never forget, something that sings down through time to us who listen today.

> *Those who wait for the Lord shall renew their strength,*
> *they shall mount up with wings like eagles,*
> *they shall run and not be weary.*
> *they shall walk and not faint.*

It is impossible to hear these words without feeling their life-giving quality. They speak to anyone who is feeling weary and despondent in the face of problems, stresses, anxieties, loss.

Psalm

Today in the sciences there is a search for a unified theory of everything. One is tempted to say that these men and women of the Bible have already shown us such a theory — "all things are unified in God."

The psalmist begins by directing us to praise God and then gives us the reasons why we should. His reasons cover all aspects of life. Maybe it would be helpful to consider them one by one.

The Lord rebuilds Jerusalem. The well-being of any society depends on its relationship with God. We live in a society that is beginning to wonder if, in abandoning its spiritual heritage, it has lost something of the utmost importance.

[The Lord] gathers the exiles of Israel ... lifts up the lowly, but casts the wicked to the ground. God demands justice in society and encourages every effort made towards it.

[God] heals the brokenhearted. God can be a source of mental and spiritual healing to those who are prepared to seek it.

[God] counts the number of the stars. Behind and within the whole creation there is design and purpose because it springs from a creating God.

[God] covers the heavens with clouds, and prepares rain for the earth; He makes grass to grow upon the mountains and green plants to serve [us all]. The environmental processes all around us are essentially divine. This is why we must acknowledge an authority in these processes, and refrain from seeing them as merely matter for our use or even exploitation.

[God] is not impressed by the might of a horse; He has no pleasure in [human] strength. God demands more than a life of exterior energy and self-celebration. God also demands that we live an interior life, growing beyond the celebration of self to the praise of God.

Second Reading

Paul is on the defensive. Some in the Corinthian community have been brutally critical of him. Some question his motives.

In today's language, they are wondering what is in it for Paul. Some are dismissing him as a big ego. Such thoughts are implied in the opening sentences of the reading.

Some are also making ugly accusations about money. Again, using today's language, they are wondering if this fellow is on the make. Paul replies that he has been trying hard to offer something free of charge, probably because he knew that such accusations were very likely to come from this troubled and fractious community. However, when he adds, *so as not to make full use of my rights in the gospel,* he is affirming his right to ask support from those whom he is trying to serve. Obviously Paul is not easily intimidated by a cranky congregation.

Paul now strikes back at his critics. He lists the ways that he has given of himself utterly. When he has been seeking to reach out to every conceivable kind of person or class or culture, he has never hesitated to speak their language, to adopt their life style, to identify with their attitudes — in a word, to blend in with them as much as possible. All this for one single reason — to reach them on behalf of Christ. You can almost hear the passion with which Paul writes: *I do it all for the sake of the gospel.*

I do it all for the sake of the gospel. The words bring us up short as we read them. To what degree are we able to say this about our own work and life? What are the motivations that drive us to do what we do, to build what we build, to expend our abilities and energy? How much self is involved in what we do? Most of us will not find it easy to answer such questions.

The Gospel

As soon as they left the synagogue. We look at the verses just before this passage begins to see what happened in the synagogue. There we find Jesus in a crowd, coping with a sudden outburst. The moment also calls for a healing on his part. All this is exhausting.

Now Jesus leaves the synagogue only to find more claims being made on his energy. It might appear that among friends and followers he could relax, but here, too, there is human need. Simon's mother-in-law is sick with a fever. Jesus goes to her, takes her hand, lifts her. The fever is cured. By our Lord's own word to us in another incident, we know that these healings have a cost for him. When a woman touched him in a crowd, he was aware of the touch because, as he said, *power has gone out from me.* Power must have gone from him in the synagogue. Power must have gone from him again in healing Peter's mother-in-law.

Now we see further demands. That evening at sundown they bring to him all who are sick or possessed with demons. We can only assume that by the time darkness falls our Lord is utterly exhausted. Yet next morning while it is still dark, he gets up and goes out to a deserted place to pray. I find myself wondering why he got up. Did he sleep badly after the exertions of the day? Was there only one thing to do — get up, find some solitude, offer to God the exhaustion that he feels? I see him turning to the source of all his human energy, the source of his humanity itself, and acknowledging the limitations of this human condition he has freely taken upon himself.

None of us is a stranger to periodic exhaustion. It is immensely grace-giving to know that in this experience our Lord is our companion. Even when in our exhaustion we give way to a natural human expletive like, "God, I'm so tired!" we are quite probably echoing the words of our Lord. To realize this is to have him beside us, and to have him beside us is to be able to draw on his grace.

Those who experienced our Lord's healing grace in Capernaum drew on Jesus in his humanity. But in our times of need we draw on a source that is no longer limited by being in human form. The Lord we turn to in our need has no limitations.

Sixth Sunday after the Epiphany: Proper 6

2 Kings 5:1–14
Psalm 30
I Corinthians 9:24–27
Mark 1:40–45

Weavings

The good news in all of today's readings is that we can cooperate with God in our own healing; indeed, our cooperation is essential to our healing.

In the first reading Naaman is healed because, with all his power, he has the good sense to listen to the voice of a slave. The psalmist says that God healed him when he cried to God for help. In the second reading Paul writes of the discipline that is essential to both our physical and our spiritual life. In the gospel, a leper's first step towards healing is recognizing that our Lord can be a resource for him.

Reflections

First Reading

I wonder why the eighteenth or nineteenth century failed to see an opera in the story of Naaman. I hear Naaman as the bass,

Elisha as the tenor, and Naaman's wife and her maid as the mezzo and the soprano. Apologies if this seems too frivolous!

Every moment of the opening sentence resounds with power, authority, and strength, but there is a note of cynicism about Naaman's triumphs. His success has depended upon military results — *By him, the Lord had given victory to Aram* — and the minute he fails to achieve a victory, he will fall from favour. His position depends not on respect or relationship, but merely on performance. In any organization, ancient army or modern corporation, this is to guarantee stress. Is this why Naaman has developed leprosy? His sickness negates his power: *The man, though a mighty warrior, suffered from leprosy.*

The atmosphere changes. From the battlefield we move to the boudoir. We meet a young woman who is a slave in Naaman's vast household. As a captured slave and a woman, she is, in her master's eyes, less than a piece of furniture. It is measure of his desperation that he listens when his wife tells him what the slave woman has suggested.

It must have taken courage for Naaman to go to the king, confess that he has leprosy, and ask for time off to deal with the problem. The situation must have been both fearful and humiliating for him. His strength and power are useless; he is no longer in control. The king is all cooperation, anxious to protect his investment in an unusually skilled general. Does Naaman need anything? Money? Bodyguards? Would a letter to the king of Israel be helpful? Both the king and Naaman are thoroughly modern — any problem can be fixed if you can find the right people and throw enough money at it — *ten talents of silver, six thousand shekels of gold, and ten sets of garments.* This is a far cry from what the slave girl had in mind when she spoke of *a prophet in Samaria.*

In some ways Naaman's arrival at the court of the king of Israel is funny. When Naaman presents his letter, the king of

Israel sees the whole thing as a political plot. The king of Aram demands that the Israelite king heal his general of leprosy, knowing that this is impossible. Then he will blame the king of Israel for refusing to do the impossible, thereby fabricating an excuse to invade. Naaman must have been astonished and dismayed at the Israelite king's response to a genuine request.

Into the confusion and cynicism of the moment comes the calm, simple message from Elisha. *Let him come to me, that he may learn that there is a prophet in Israel.* Even this self-important general may discover that there is an authority not based on naked power.

So Naaman and his entourage arrive at the house of Elisha. What happens is utterly unexpected. Elisha doesn't even appear. Instead he sends a messenger, who tells Naaman to go jump in the river! Naaman interprets this seeming frivolity as contemptuous and is enraged: *I thought that for me* — notice that *for me* — *he would surely come out, and stand, and call upon the name of the Lord his God, and would wave his hand over the spot, and cure the leprosy.* He sweeps away in anger.

But just as Naaman was earlier assisted by a servant, so at this moment he is assisted by another servant, a very courageous man who, with support from others, persuades him to reconsider. Notice the flattery — the servant knows him well. *Father, if the prophet had commanded you to do something difficult, would you not have done it? How much more, when all he said to you was, 'Wash, and be clean'?*

In the last scene Naaman stands, as he was bidden, in the Jordan, dipping in the cool water seven times. Then he looks down at his body to see that the flesh *is restored like the flesh of a young boy, and he [is] clean.*

Personal authority has bowed its head in obedience to a greater and more mysterious authority. Pride has given way to humility. Power has recognized its own vulnerability. A personality that has tended to mistake itself for a god has come into the presence of the reality of God. After all this has occurred, healing has become possible.

The Psalm

The psalm echoes the first reading, describing in vivid and unforgettable terms an experience like Naaman's.

To recognize the sequence, it might be well to begin with the lines, *While I felt secure, I said, "I shall never be disturbed." You, Lord, with your favour, made me as strong as the mountains.* Someone is feeling immensely confident about life, able to handle anything with his own resources. Suddenly everything changes. *I cried to you, O Lord ... O Lord, be my helper.* Something ghastly has happened that may even be life-threatening. It sweeps away all the self-confidence and makes the person realize exactly how vulnerable he is. Recovery follows, with all the joy and gratitude that goes with it. *You have turned my wailing into dancing.*

It will be a long time before the person can say again with self-assurance, *I shall never be disturbed.* From now on there will be an awareness of dependence on God. *O Lord my God, I will give you thanks for ever.*

Second Reading

In this passage, is the older Paul remembering his youth when he attended the Greek games in Tarsus? Is it possible that he himself was a runner? Was there a moment when he stood — in those days runners did not crouch as they do today — at the start of a race, heart pounding, hoping that the weeks of training would pay off? Or was there a moment when he faced a boxing opponent, ready for anything? We will never know, but even to ask the questions makes it possible to clothe this distant intellectual and spiritual giant with a little humanity!

Paul is speaking of the spirit in images of the physical: *Run in such a way that you may win it.* This is good advice about anything in life. The will to win need not necessarily require beating or dominating others. It is the self with whom we compete — will against desire, discipline against appetite, the ability to stay focused against the tendency to be easily distracted. In arenas like these we train to run the race of the spiritual journey. God demands our involvement, our decisions, our choices, our effort, our commitment. It is essential that we *do not run aimlessly ... nor [do we] box as though beating the air.* We focus on the goal and strive to win.

The Gospel

It is easy to forget that a very real added terror of leprosy in ancient times was loneliness. Contagion meant banishment from home, from community, from the touch of those whom you loved, from the voices of friends. There was even a ghastly measurement by which you were legally isolated — one hundred and fifty yards from any other human being other than a fellow leper. This is why I wonder how many previous attempts this man had made to approach our Lord. Why did he take the risk? Had he heard that this man would not back away in horror?

There is desperation in every word of the opening sentence. The man comes begging and kneeling. He has lost all dignity, all ability to control feelings. No wonder our Lord is moved with pity. His gesture is simple — *Jesus stretched out his hand and touched him* — yet it spanned the vast gulf between health and disease. To touch this leper was to pierce through the normal fear, loathing, and revulsion, and to challenge them. In our own times, it moved people's hearts that Diana Princess of Wales reached out and touched patients suffering with AIDS. Her gesture challenged the fears that isolate sufferers and add immeasurably to the burden of illness.

Notice the momentary sequence of this healing.

Jesus stretched out his hand ...
touched him ...
said — I do choose....

Here is all that we need to do and be when we respond to the vulnerability and the need of another. Our Lord is generous of gesture and warm of speech. Every movement, every nuance of voice conveys caring. Such things can make an incalculable difference in tending illness.

In this passage, when he came to Jesus, the sick man took the initiative, the first step towards his own healing. Notice the immense trust implied in the statement, *If you choose, you can make me clean.* As a Christian, I am being reminded that, although my own trust is fragile, our Lord can be a source of healing to me if only I turn to him.

Seventh Sunday after the Epiphany: Proper 7

Isaiah 43:18–25
Psalm 41
2 Corinthians 1:18–22
Mark 2:1–12

Weavings

The wonderful theme of today's passages can be expressed in three words: God is faithful.

In the first reading we hear Isaiah insisting that God is faithful in spite of every shortcoming of God's people. The psalmist echoes this theme by singing a hymn to the faithfulness of God. In the second reading Paul is emphasizing exactly the same thing to his readers in Corinth, this time referring to Jesus. In the gospel passage we see Jesus continuing — in other words, remaining faithful to — his healing ministry in spite of all the carping and criticism around him.

Reflections

First Reading

Do not remember the former things, or consider the things of old. Perhaps Isaiah is looking at the ruins of the city with some people gathered around him. What they see is ugly and dispiriting. They have dreamed of this place and this day. Now they see the actuality, and it is appalling. Isaiah is trying to make sure that they do not dwell on it and become incapable of applying themselves to the task to be accomplished.

Then Isaiah sounds the very opposite theme. He suggests that God is saying, "I am about to do a new thing." He points beyond the ruins to where there are signs in nature of new growth. *Now it springs forth, do you not perceive it?* Farther and farther he lifts their gaze, beyond the ruined city, over the neighbouring hills, out to the wilderness. It is as if God is saying, *I will make a way in the wilderness and rivers in the desert.* Notice how Isaiah ends this thought with an affectionate phrase: *my chosen people, the people whom I formed for myself.*

However, although the people must be comforted, they must also be called to respond. Why were they chosen by God? *So that they might declare my praise,* says God.

Now comes a stern reminder: *Yet you did not call upon me … You have been weary of me, O Israel.* The people's unworthy response is catalogued harshly. But in spite of their having deeply disappointed God, the response will be a magnanimity that emerges from the nature of the God who endlessly forgives. *I am He who blots out your transgressions for my own sake.*

These words of encouragement were addressed to a people facing the awesome task of bringing their city and nation back to life. They address us, too, as we are called to bring the church once again to life and hope and strength.

The Psalm

The psalmist's abundant enemies are present as threatening and even terrifying voices. *All my enemies whisper together about me and devise evil against me ... Even my best friend, whom I trusted, has lifted up his heel and turned against me.*

Enemies are so present in the psalms that one has to decide what their presence means for us who recite these verses today. While it is true that not one of us is without those who do not like us or particularly wish us well, it is also true that most of us have few real enemies who actually wish us harm. For us, at least some of the enemies that appear in the psalms must surely be those enemies that we give birth to inside ourselves. Everyone knows the inner voice that begins to speak when we have some physical ailment, a recurring pain, or an inconclusive medical test: a *deadly thing ... has fastened on [me].*

The opening verses offer an antidote to the poison of inner enemies. To consider the poor and needy is somehow healing and energizing for those who do so. It seems that giving is in some mysterious way twice blessed by a faithful God — blessing the receiver and the giver. A readiness to give to others sweetens life and gives healing against the many acids that can corrode it.

Second Reading

Once again Paul is on the defensive. It seems that he was unable to keep his promise to visit the Christian community in Corinth. As a result, they are lashing out at him, accusing him of saying one thing and meaning another. This is why the passage starts off so vehemently. *As surely as God is faithful, our word to you has not been "Yes and No."* Because of the way he stays with the subject of Yes-and-No, I suspect that this same phrase must have been used about Paul. He rejects the accusation of being a Yes-and-No person by saying that the Christ he preaches is not a Yes-and-No person: *In him it is always "Yes."* Paul passionately drives the point home: *In him every one of God's promises is a "Yes."*

Paul now seizes the opportunity to make a much bigger point. He seems to say to these Corinthian Christians, "Look, there is much more at stake here than just the relationship between us, with its ups and downs like any other human relationship. The important thing is this: *it is God who establishes us with you in Christ.* Or, "God has brought us together. We have a sense of sharing God's Spirit, and this is only a beginning!"

Once again we hear the theme of these readings. Human beings have their successes and failures in relationships, but God remains faithful.

The Gospel

Jesus is teaching in Capernaum. The listening crowd is so huge that it bars access to him. A group of friends is determined to bring to this renowned healer someone in great need. They go up the outside steps of the house, literally break through the thatch and hardened mud of the roof, and lower the man into the presence of our Lord.

Almost as if he wishes to challenge certain people who are present, Jesus says to the sick man, *Son, your sins are forgiven.* There is consternation among some in the crowd. God alone forgives sins! What is this fellow claiming? There follows what was probably a harsh confrontation. The serious charge of blasphemy is sounded. Jesus does not give an inch. When the hubbub has died down, he turns to the sick man and heals him of his affliction.

Consider the contrast between those who bring the sick man and those who are ready to condemn. One group is utterly determined to believe that Jesus can respond to their need. The other group is equally determined to condemn Jesus, including his ability to heal. Consider also the contrast between the attitude of those who spurn Jesus, and the attitude of Jesus himself. His detractors criticize and condemn his ministry of healing. What is our Lord's response? To walk away? To deprive those in need of his gifts merely because he receives criticism and insults? No. He responds by continuing his healing. In the face of the human rejection, the divine response is generosity. In the face of the human No, the divine word remains Yes. We recall Isaiah's insistence that God is faithful, and Paul's, that Jesus' constant word is Yes, not No.

Eighth Sunday after the Epiphany: Proper 7

Hosea 2:14–20
Psalm 103:1–13, 22
2 Corinthians 3:1–6
Mark 2:13–22

Weavings

In all of these scriptures a determined love is offered, in spite of all that might be expected to crush it.

In the first reading Hosea acts as the mouth of a loving God who remains faithful to a people that has been far from faithful. In the second reading we hear Paul expressing his unflagging devotion to a community that has been nothing short of hurtful to him. In the gospel our Lord explains why, in spite of criticism, he insists on offering friendship to the outcasts of his society. The psalmist echoes all this by singing of a God who forgives, heals, and redeems a difficult people.

Reflections

First Reading

Hosea's language is not just loving but erotic: *I will now allure her, and bring her into the wilderness, and speak tenderly to her ... There she shall respond as in the days of her youth.*

Yet this passage is not about a human love affair, although there were very human reasons for Hosea to express the thoughts of God in this way. He himself may have experienced the breakdown of a marriage or, at least, the long and tortured endurance of a relationship gone sour. He longs passionately for reconciliation. So when he begins to agonize about another relationship, that between his people and their God, he naturally slips into language that serves both concerns in his mind. The statement, *On that day, says the Lord, you will call me "My husband," and no longer will you call me "My Baal,"* may come from the possibility that Hosea's wife, Gomar, was involved in the shadowed world of religious prostitution. Certainly many people in the society were so involved.

In the first two chapters of this book, it is difficult to tell whether Hosea is speaking of his marriage or of the marriage between God and this people. He may be telling us merely that his marriage has to be lived in a society that has betrayed its relationship with God and has become a kind of whore, in the sense of having given allegiance to other pagan gods such as Baal.

We who read this passage today are moved by the passionate way in which God's love for the people is expressed. We hear God say, *I will take you for my wife forever,* as a promise of a renewed relationship.

This promise is much larger than any relationship the people can find with the pagan Baal. With Baal there will be the cyclic celebrations of the seasons, the fertility cultic celebrations with their mingling of wild sexuality and brutal sacrifice. With God there will be a covenant. In Hosea's language, it will be a marriage. *I will take you for my wife in faithfulness; and you shall know the Lord.*

Look at the magnificent terms of this covenant. It is offered between the human and the natural order: *with the wild animals, the birds of the air, and the creeping things of the ground.* It will be a covenant of peace among people and societies: *I will abolish the bow, the sword, and war from the land.* Finally, it will offer a moral order of justice, righteousness, love, and mercy.

These are the very terms in which we are searching for a worldwide covenant in our own time. Is it possible that as a culture we have gone whoring after other gods, as Hosea would have said? What gods might they be?

The Psalm

There are moments in life when every one of us, whether we know it or not, sings this psalm. These are moments when we are overcome with the wish to express sheer joy in being alive: *Bless the Lord, O my soul, and all that is within me, bless his holy name.* When something has been achieved which we know well was not achieved by ourselves alone: *forget not all his benefits.* When we realize that we are free from something that has been eating at us for a long time: *he forgives all your sins and heals all your infirmities.* When we are given a new lease on life by the passing of some dreaded threat: *he redeems your life from the grave.* When there comes an intensely physical moment with a sense of life itself coursing through your body: *He satisfies you with good things, and your youth is renewed like an eagle's.*

Now the psalmist teaches us that what can be true personally can also be true societally. *The Lord executes righteousness and judgement for all who are oppressed.* As God is merciful to an individual, so there will be mercy for the wrongs of a society: *[God] has not dealt with us according to our sins.* There are, however, conditions to be met. God's mercy is *upon those who fear him ... On those who keep his covenant and remember his commandments and do them.*

From his own life to the life of a people — so goes the thinking of the psalmist. What a far cry from the modern tendency to remain in the realm of the self, to see self as essentially alone amid countless other selves. The psalmist offers us the gift of a corporate consciousness, the ability to see ourselves as part of a living body, certainly composed of unique other selves, but all directed and drawn to a reality beyond themselves, a reality the psalmist would call God. *The Lord has set his throne in heaven, and his kingdom has dominion over all.* For the psalmist, this is the vision that ultimately ennobles and enriches the individual soul, making it cry out, *bless the Lord, O my soul.*

Second Reading

Are we beginning to commend ourselves again? Surely we do not need, as some do, letters of recommendation to you or from you, do we? I hear this as a mingling of sadness and sarcasm. His relationship with Corinth has probably cost Paul more emotionally and mentally than that with any other community. It would appear that they are now asking for letters of recommendation, as if they did not already know Paul. This must have been extremely hurtful to him, and he is saying in effect, "Surely it has not come to this between us."

Now, instead of an angry outburst — which would not have surprised us from Paul — there is a simply beautiful remark. *You yourselves are our letter, written on our hearts, to be known and read by all.* Paul takes the sore point of a request for letters and turns it into a compliment, almost an endearment towards the very people who have hurt him.

He tells them that he is proud of them and of the community that together he and they have brought into being. *You are a letter of Christ, prepared by us, written not with ink but with the Spirit of the living God.* I suspect that there were some glistening eyes and some shame-faced expressions as this was being read out in the Corinthian community. The lovely images and language continue: *[This] letter of Christ ... has been written not on tablets of stone but on tablets of human hearts.*

As he does so often, Paul attributes his own success to God. Then, turning again to the idea of a letter, he makes a wonderful play on words. This new covenant from Jesus Christ is *not of letter but of spirit; for the letter kills, but the Spirit gives life.* Paul, the great pastor, has been hurt, but he determinedly transforms injury into blessing.

The Gospel

He saw Levi ... sitting at the tax booth. Anyone else would have been filled with loathing. Not Jesus. He sees something in this man that no one else sees. By now, because of what he does for a living, Levi is probably lonely, abrasive, and thick-skinned. He has had to develop a personal armour, impervious to insults and endless confrontations about money. Yet Levi *got up and followed him.* Did he give up being a tax collector? The text does not say so. Perhaps he became a different kind of tax collector. We cannot know one way or the other, but the possibilities are intriguing.

We find ourselves now at a dinner in Levi's house, and I suspect it was a very good dinner. Around the table are some familiar faces, disciples already with Jesus. But the rest are tax people. The word must have gone out that someone appreciates them enough not to write them off as scoundrels and exploiters.

Jesus is careful never to write people off in classes or occupations or types or lifestyles. A man or woman is treated and accepted as he or she is. Levi is not an object called a tax gatherer, but a potential disciple. However, acceptance of the person does not mean acceptance of what the person does. When the charge comes that he is eating with sinners, our Lord acknowledges this possibility. *Those who are well have no need of a physician ... I have come to call not the righteous but sinners.*

The theme of this Sunday appears again here. The God of Israel loves in the face of betrayal and rejection. Paul speaks affectionately and affirmingly in spite of insult. Our Lord continues to be open, affirming, hospitable, accepting, in spite of criticism. After dinner he is questioned again in a carping, manipulative way. He knows well the question about fasting is not asked to gain information or to learn anything. It is asked as a trap. Yet he answers without a hint of confrontation or dismissal. Instead he offers truths about life that these people ignore at their peril. *No one puts new wine into old wineskins; otherwise the wine will burst the skins.* Wisdom is offered in exchange for criticism, acceptance in exchange for condemnation, friendship in exchange for enmity.

Last Sunday after the Epiphany: The Transfiguration

2 Kings 2:1–12
Psalm 50:1–6
2 Corinthians 4:3–6
Mark 9:2–9

Weavings

In each of today's readings a light begins to blaze from a person, transfiguring the way in which that person is perceived by others. It could be said that it is the other's perception that is transfigured.

In the first reading the young Elisha perceives the real nature of his relationship with the older Elijah only in the last moment of their being together. In the psalm the very ordinary city of Zion or Jerusalem suddenly becomes a place of light when it is regarded as the dwelling place of God. In the second reading Paul presents the good news as that from which the light of Christ shines. In the gospel the disciples see Jesus as they have never seen him before — clothed in light, transfigured.

Reflections

First Reading

This passage describes how one person helps another to mature and to see things he had not seen before about himself, about the person trying to help him, and about life itself. The older Elijah helps the younger Elisha to achieve this understanding.

For some years now a struggle has threatened to divide the nation. The struggle is about two ways of understanding God, thereby understanding all of reality. One way — or as they would say, one god —is the god called Baal. To worship Baal is to see all of reality in terms of the cycles of nature — the seasons, the cycles of the sun and the moon, the menstrual cycle, seedtime, harvest. To worship Yahweh is to think of God as a God of history. To think in this way is to see time as linear rather than cyclic. We might say that life is more a progress than a treadmill. In some ways Baal and Yahweh are always struggling in the human mind and heart.

In this struggle Elijah has been the great champion of Yahweh, but he realizes that he is growing old and has not long to live. For some time he has been training a younger man to take his place. But Elijah realizes that there is very little time left and Elisha is far from ready. At this juncture we move into the passage set for today.

Notice the pattern of three. Three times the older man tries to disengage. Three times the younger man will not let him. Every time the older man tries to detach himself from the younger, Elisha's reply reveals a great deal. I hear his repeated statement, *As the Lord lives, and as you yourself live, I will not leave you,* as a plea to the older man not to die.

The school of the prophets at Jericho echo Elisha's fears. All of us have had the experience of fearing something that we do not wish to acknowledge, while knowing deep down that we must wrestle with it. Elisha desperately tries to silence those voices. *Be silent,* he says, again and again.

There comes the moment when the older man knows there is no more time. In a final question he confronts the younger man with the reality of the situation after they have crossed the river. *Tell me what I may do for you, before I am taken from you.* The reply is a desperate plea: *Please let me inherit a double share of your spirit.* What Elisha does not realize is that he must find the spirit within himself. No one can give it to him.

Elijah's reply is magnificent in its wisdom and insight. *You have asked a hard thing.* He means it is an impossible thing, but Elijah is too kind to say so. Then he says: *If you see me as I am being taken from you, it will be granted you; if not, it will not.* He means something like this: "I cannot give you something that you do not already have yourself, but if you are prepared and able to face my death, then you will discover within yourself the spirit of courage and wisdom that you long for. It is up to you now."

And so the time of Elijah's death comes. When it comes, the feelings of the younger man pour out in the cry he gives: *Father, father! The chariots of Israel and its horsemen!* For him the older man has been everything — strength, wisdom, security.

Traditionally we see here the transfiguration of Elijah, swept in a whirlwind up to heaven. At Jesus' transfiguration the disciples saw Elijah appear with Moses and talk with Jesus. But I think we also see here the transfiguration of Elisha, who in that moment saw things in a new way. He moved from immaturity and dependence to maturity and independence, a transfiguration that all of us must experience at some time in our lives if we are to be full and complete human beings.

The Psalm

The Chinook is a phenomenon of the foothills of the Rockies. For most of the day the winter sky will be overcast. Then, beginning in the west, a great arch of clear sky will form. It pushes the dark clouds eastward. Finally, as the suns moves towards setting, it suddenly appears below the line of dark cloud, blazing and pouring over the land. There is a flood of light. If you are driving or looking west, your eyes are assaulted by the brightness.

In these lines of the psalm I see this moment of the sun's appearing. For the psalmist there are times when the brightness of God's glory blazes out and brooks no response other than a bowing down in humility and awe. *Out of Zion, perfect in its beauty, God reveals himself in glory.* In such moments there is nothing intimate, nothing domestic, about God. *Before him there is a consuming flame, and round about him a raging storm.*

God himself is judge. In the Chinook, at the moment of blazing light, there is a sense of being surrounded by glory and beauty immeasurably greater than oneself, and in this sense one feels measured or judged. Likewise, when the light of God blazes within our personal experience, there is a sense of being illumined by a presence infinitely greater than oneself. In this presence the poverty of self is revealed, felt, and in this sense, judged.

Second Reading

We continue with this difficult letter to the Corinthian Christians in which Paul receives a criticism from the community. He is accused of being deliberately obscure and deceiving in the way he communicates the Christian message.

Paul is deeply hurt, and it shows in the way he responds. He takes the charge and throws it back. *Even if our gospel is veiled, it is veiled to those who are perishing.* Paul is saying that those in the community who charge him are doing so to deliberately harm his work and the gospel.

Another criticism surfaces. Paul is accused of building a personal empire. To this he vehemently replies, *We do not proclaim ourselves; we proclaim Jesus Christ as Lord.* Then almost bitterly he adds, *We proclaim ... ourselves as your slaves for Jesus' sake.*

Because he is stung by this criticism, Paul finds it difficult to move on. He brilliantly turns to an Old Testament image — the moment when God brings light from darkness in the process of creation. I hear Paul saying something like this.

Suppose it is true that there is a shadow or a darkness at the heart of my ministry to you. Suppose the things you say about me are true. Yet our own scriptures — the very scriptures we share and believe in — tell us that God can bring light from darkness. Even if there is a darkness in me, God has brought from that darkness *the light of the knowledge of the glory of God in the face of Jesus Christ.*

This last statement of Paul shows us the immense spirituality of the man. Although he is hurt by criticism, his overriding concern is still the gospel and our Lord. "Think of me what you like," we hear him say. "The only important thing is that you hear and receive what I have tried to bring you." We see a kind of light shining from Paul — the light of great courage, pastoral forbearance, and integrity.

This passage can speak to us when we ourselves are under fire. When we know that criticism comes from a wish to harm us or our work, we can continue and strengthen our efforts. We need to be prepared to spend more energy commending our work, rather than defending and justifying it. Like Paul, we can transfigure the situation from being a negative block to having a positive outcome.

The Gospel

The transfiguration of our Lord speaks deeply to our own search for personal transfiguration, and our longing for the transfiguration of both the church and the world.

I recall Helmut Thielicke saying of this passage that he did not think that anything happened to our Lord on the mountain. Whatever happened, it was within and to the disciples. Thielicke maintains that our Lord continued throughout this episode to be what he always was, the incarnation of God in human flesh, but that for a fleeting moment the eyes of the disciples were opened to the unimaginable glory of the incarnation.

I have never felt that Thielicke was in any way lessening the mystery and the truth of the transfiguration. His insight has always addressed me powerfully because it bears out my own experience as I try to relate to Jesus Christ as Lord.

For me, Jesus Christ is Lord. He is always the incarnation of God in human flesh. But for most of the time I am blinded to the glory of this truth that I believe. I worship him. I pray to him. I give thanks to him. God forgive me, for I have spent countless hours writing about him! Yet I find that most of the time I take this glory for granted. I attribute this negligence to the overall busyness of my life, to the limitations of my spirituality, and to my all too human nature. For all this, my prayer is that I will be forgiven. (As I write these things I realize how similar they are to the glosses that Irish monks used to put at the edge of the pages of their manuscripts!)

But every now and again there come moments when the blindness is lifted and, like the three disciples, I encounter my Lord transfigured. I assume it is not he who has changed but, in some mysterious way, I who have been changed, at least for a fleeting moment. It may be a moment in worship when wine is indeed more than wine. It may be a human moment — holding a grandchild in my arms and feeling immensely grateful, or looking at a crucifix that now hangs in the home of one of our children, and suddenly recalling the great cost of the Christian faith. These are moments when I realize the meaning of our Lord's transfiguring power.

At such moments I identify with what I see happening to the disciples who were present at that original moment of trans-figuration. Just as they said, *Rabbi, it is good for us to be here,* so do I want to remain in the light of his presence. Just as they did not know what to say, I find such moments beyond lan-guage. Just as they were terrified, so I feel something like terror or awe in the presence of the numinous.

Last of all, when I read that a voice said to the disciples, *This is my Son, the Beloved; listen to him,* I realize that the same words are being addressed to me, telling me to remember who Jesus Christ really is in my life and to stop taking him for granted. Insofar as this is being said to me, I find that moments of trans-figuration in my experience are also sent as correctives, as times of spiritual discipline.